GCSE RELIGIOUS STUDIES
FOR WJEC B – UNIT 2

# RELIGION AND HUMAN EXPERIENCE

## BASED ON CHRISTIANITY AND ISLAM

WJEC
CBAC

INA TAYLOR

OXFORD
UNIVERSITY PRESS

## Acknowledgements

p.8 (left) © Sipa Press/Rex Features, (right) © David Pearson/Alamy; p.9 (top) © PA/PA Archive/Press Association Images, (middle) © Tryphosa Ho/Alamy, (bottom) © iStockphoto.com/Craig DeBourbon; p.10 (top) © Jeff J Mitchell/Reuters/Corbis, (bottom) © Steve Lovegrove. Image from BigStockPhoto.com; p.11 (top) © AP/Empics, (middle) © Corbis/Reuters, (bottom) © RSPCA Photolibrary; p.12 © Corbis/Reuters; p.13 © Mary Evans Picture Library; p.14 © Ark Religion.com/Helene Rogers; p.15 Islamic Relief Worldwide; p.16 © Adrian Brooks/Rex Features; p.17 (top left) Courtesy of Ina Taylor, (top right, middle, bottom middle, bottom right) Muslim Aid; p.20 © Sipa Press/Rex Features; p.21 © Rex Features; p.22 © PA/PA Archive/Press Association Images; p.23 © Danny Lawson/PA Archive/PA Photos; p.26 © Tony Kyriacou/Rex Features; p.27 © iStockphoto.com/Craig DeBourbon; p.28 © Tryphosa Ho/Alamy; p.29 (top) © James Jim James/PA Archive/Press Association Images, (middle) © Mike Booth/Alamy; p.30 © 2004 TopFoto/Woodmansterne; p.31 © Kazuyoshi Nomachi/Corbis; p.32 © David Pearson/Alamy; p.33 © David Turnley/Corbis; p.34 © EAPPI/Thomas Meier; p.35 © EAPPI; p.37 (left) © Sipa Press/Rex Features, (top middle) © David Pearson/Alamy, (bottom middle) © iStockphoto.com/Craig DeBourbon, (top right) © PA/PA Archive/Press Association Images, (bottom left) © Tryphosa Ho/Alamy; p.38 (left) © Ferdaus Shamim/Sygma/Corbis, (right) © Geoffrey Robinson/Rex Features; p.39 (top) © Shout/Rex Features, (middle) © Tissuepix/Science Photo Library, (bottom) © Stephen Boitano/Reuters/Corbis; p.40 © Shout/Rex Features; p.41 © iStockphoto.com/Sandy Jones; p.42 (left) © iStockphoto.com/Elena Elisseeva, (right) © iStockphoto.com/Alejandro Rivera; p.43 (left) © iStockphoto.com/Wilson Valentin, (right) © iStockphoto.com/Jill Chen; p.44 © Chris Ison/PA Archive/Press Association Images; p.45 (top) © Rex Features, (bottom) © Rex Features; p.48 © Steve Allen/Science Photo Library; p.49 © John Duricka/AP/PA Photos; p.50 © Eva-Lotta Jansson/Corbis; p.51 © Stephen Boitano/Reuters/Corbis; p.52 © Peter Sanders; p.53 © Tissuepix/Science Photo Library; p.54 © Ferdaus Shamim/Sygma/Corbis; p.55 © Getty Images; p.58 © Penny Tweedie/Alamy; p.59 Courtesy of Ina Taylor; p.61 © Reuters/Corbis; p.62 © Mauro Fermariello/Science Photo Library; p.62 © Geoffrey Robinson/Rex Features; p.64 © Jacek Bednarczyk/epa/Corbis; p.65 © newsteam.co.uk; p.67 (top left) © Ferdaus Shamim/Sygma/Corbis, (bottom left) © Shout/Rex Features, (middle) © Geoffrey Robinson/Rex Features, (top right) © Stephen Boitano/Reuters/Corbis, (bottom right) © Tissuepix/Science Photo Library; p.68 (left) © Ivan Sekretarev/AP/Press Association Images, (right) © Francis Dean/Rex Features; p.69 (top) © Alamy/Joe Fox, (middle) © Dave Penman/Rex Features, (bottom) © David Butcher/ArkReligion.com/Alamy; p.70 (top) © David Butcher/ArkReligion.com/Alamy, (middle) © Jens Dresling/AP/Press Association Images, (bottom) © SCPhotos/Alamy; p.71 © Ivan Sekretarev/AP/Press Association Images, (middle) © iStockphoto.com/wando studios, (bottom) © Jim West/Alamy; p.72 (top) (top) CAFOD (Catholic Agency for Overseas Development), www.cafod.co.uk, (bottom) © Catherine Ogolla/CAFOD; p.73 (top left) © Claire Goudsmit/CAFOD, (top right) © Kate Stanworth/CAFOD, (bottom left) © Richard Wainwright/CAFOD, (bottom right) © Claire Goudsmit/CAFOD; p.74 Islamic Relief Worldwide; p.75 (top, bottom) Islamic Relief Worldwide; p.78 © Nigel Roddis/epa/Corbis; p.79 © Dave Penman/Rex Features; p.80 © iStockphoto.com/naheed choudhry; p.80–81 © AFP/Getty Images; p.82 © Nic Cleave Photography/Alamy; p.83 © Jeff Morgan religion/Alamy; p.84 © Pascal Deloche/Godong/Corbis; p.85 © SCPhotos/Alamy; p.88 Courtesy of Ina Taylor; p.89 (top) © Francis Dean/Rex Features, (bottom) Courtesy of Ina Taylor; p.90 © Mohammad Hamza Mian/Alamy; p.90–91 © United Archives GmbH/Alamy; p.92 (top) © Bradford District Faiths Forum (BDFF), (middle) © Bradford District Faiths Forum (BDFF)/Michelle Heseltine, (bottom) © Bradford District Faiths Forum (BDFF)/Tim Garthwaite; p.93 (top) © Bradford District Faiths Forum (BDFF)/Michelle Heseltine, (bottom) © Bradford District Faiths Forum (BDFF)/Michelle Heseltine; p.94 © Alamy/Joe Fox; p.95 (top) © Kelly Kerr/AP/Press Association Images, (bottom) © Jenny Matthews/Alamy; p.97 (left) © Ivan Sekretarev/AP/Press Association Images, (top middle) © Francis Dean/Rex Features, (bottom middle) © Alamy/Joe Fox, (top right) © Dave Penman/Rex Features, (bottom right) © David Butcher/ArkReligion.com/Alamy; p.98 (left) © Sipa Press/Rex Features, (right) © iStockphoto.com/MBPHOTO; p.99 (top) © Dag Ohrlund/Rex Features, (middle) © Art Directors, (bottom) © Stephen Kelly/PA Archive/PA Photos; p.101 © Anup Shah/naturepl.com; p.102 © Art Directors; p.103 (top) © ArkReligion.com/Helene Rogers, (bottom) © iStockphoto.com/Floortje; p.104 © Sipa Press/Rex Features; p.109 © iStockphoto.com/William Mahar; p.110 © Eamonn Clarke/allaction.co.uk /Eamonn and James Clarke/EMPICS Entertainment/PA Photos; p.112 © Dag Ohrlund/Rex Features; p.113 © Digital Stock; p.114 © ArkReligion.com; p.115 © Getty Images/AFP; p.118 © iStockphoto.com/MBPHOTO; p.119 © Art Directors; p.120 © Stephen Kelly/PA Archive/PA Photos; p.121 © Angie Zelter; p.122 © Louise Batalla Duran/Alamy; p.123 Islamic Relief Worldwide; p.124 © Adisa/Fotolia; p.125 © Voisin/Phanie/Rex Features

p.22 CAFOD (Catholic Agency for Overseas Development), www.cafod.co.uk; p.23 © Britain Yearly Meeting, Friends House, 173 Euston Road, NW1 2BJ; p.34 © Britain Yearly Meeting, Friends House, 173 Euston Road, NW1 2BJ; p.44 Extract from the General Medical Council (GMC), Good Medical Practice (2006); p.45 Source: 'Jehovah's Witness mother dies after refusing blood', Times Online, 5/11/2007 © 2008 Times Newspapers Ltd; p.50 Quotes from the Catechism of the Catholic Church are taken from www.vatican.va © Libreria Editrice Vaticana; p.51 *Abortion: A briefing paper* from Church of England, www.cofe.anglican.org; p.59 Quotes from the Catechism of the Catholic Church are taken from www.vatican.va © Libreria Editrice Vaticana; p.65 Source: 'Why Daniel James chose to die', Times Online, 19/10/2008 © 2009 Times Newspapers Ltd; p.100 Copyright © United Nations 2009; p.111 © Amnesty International Publications, 1 Easton Street, London WC1X 0DW, United Kingdom, www.amnesty.org; p.120 Adapted from: 'Catholic priest will risk jail to protect asylum seeker', Ekklesia, 01/11/2008 and 'Faith news', Times Online, 06/11/2004; p.124 Adapted from: 'Muslim checkout staff get an alcohol opt-out clause', The Times, 30/09/2007 and 'Sainsbury allows Muslim cashiers to refuse to sell alcoholic beverages', Islam Today, 03/09/2007; p.125 Difficult descisions for Hanif' based on 'When faith and medicine collide', BBC Berkshire, 30/05/2008

Bible scriptures are taken from the *Good News Bible*, published by The Bible Societies/Collins © American Bible Society.

Quotes from the Qur'an are taken from *The Koran: With parallel Arabic text*, trans. N. J. Dawood, published by Penguin (1995).

Quotes from the Catechism of the Catholic Church are taken from www.vatican.va © Libreria Editrice Vaticana.

# OXFORD
### UNIVERSITY PRESS

Great Clarendon Street, Oxford OX2 6DP

Oxford University Press is a department of the University of Oxford. It furthers the University's objective of excellence in research, scholarship, and education by publishing worldwide in

Oxford   New York

Auckland   Cape Town   Dar es Salaam   Hong Kong   Karachi
Kuala Lumpur   Madrid   Melbourne   Mexico City   Nairobi
New Delhi   Shanghai   Taipei   Toronto

With offices in
Argentina   Austria   Brazil   Chile   Czech Republic   France   Greece
Guatemala   Hungary   Italy   Japan   Poland   Portugal   Singapore
South Korea   Switzerland   Thailand   Turkey   Ukraine   Vietnam

Oxford is a registered trade mark of Oxford University Press
in the UK and in certain other countries

© Ina Taylor 2010

British Library Cataloguing in Publication Data

Data available

ISBN 978-1-85008-506-5

10 9 8 7 6 5 4

Printed in Malaysia by Vivar Printing Sdn Bhd.

Paper used in the production of this book is a natural, recyclable product made from wood grown in sustainable forests. The manufacturing process conforms to the environmental regulations of the country of origin.

Editor: Judi Hunter, Spellbound Books

Text design and layout: eMC Design Ltd., www.emcdesign.org.uk

Picture researchers: Sue Sharp, Cathy Hurren

Cover design: Form, www.form.uk.com

Cover image: © Getty Images (above); © iStockphoto.com/Sebastien Roche-Lochen (below)

# Contents

# Introduction

## Some helpful tips about using this book

This textbook is designed to help you prepare for the WJEC exam *GCSE Religious Studies Specification B – Unit 2*. You can choose to answer the questions in this exam from two religious traditions, which may be Christianity and another religion or two traditions within Christianity. Because Islam is the most popular religious tradition schools choose to study along with Christianity, in this book you will study the topics from a Christian and a Muslim perspective.

This course explores the relevance of religious beliefs, practices, values and traditions to some central questions and issues. Half of the course, and the exam, focus on learning and understanding the reasons people have for their beliefs and practices. The other half of the course challenges you to think about the different attitudes people have towards these issues and to come up with your own informed opinion.

## How does the book work?

The book follows the exam specification very closely. It is divided into four chapters.

### Chapter 1 Religion and conflict

In this chapter you will study religion and conflict with a particular focus on peace, forgiveness and attitudes to war. You will start by thinking about why some people suffer, especially when they don't seem to deserve it. You will then go on to look at the different attitudes Christians and Muslims have towards suffering and what they do to help. This leads you on to study different attitudes to war and why some people are pacifists. The chapter ends with an examination of the work of peace activists and attitudes towards forgiveness amongst Christians and Muslims.

### Chapter 2 Religion and medicine

This chapter is concerned with the way medical ethics impact on personal choice. You will study what is meant by sanctity of life and the role that conscience plays in making life and death choices. You will get the chance to examine some of the dilemmas people face when considering the difficult issues of abortion or euthanasia. You will examine the ethical issues raised by IVF and other medical advances, and then consider the Christian and Muslim responses to these issues. You will explore the dilemma of whether to spend money advancing medicine or on feeding the hungry.

### Chapter 3 Religious expression

This chapter examines some of the many different ways people express their faith. You will consider whether faith is a personal matter or whether it needs to be expressed through action. This will lead you on to study in-depth the work of a Christian charity and a Muslim charity. You will examine the way some members of a faith use symbols and special clothing as part of their worship, the different ways people express their faith by going on pilgrimage and will consider the value of interfaith activities and whether people should try to share their faith with others.

### Chapter 4 Authority – religion and state

This chapter challenges you to think about the impact of authority on religion and society. You will examine the issue of human rights and study in detail the life of one religious believer who worked to secure human rights for others. You will move on to look at attitudes to punishment and the death penalty, including Christian and Muslim responses. You will consider what authority Christians and Muslims turn to when they require answers to moral issues. You will end by looking at the conflict that can arise for Christians and Muslims when their personal convictions clash with other authorities.

# Topic pages

The pages have been designed with lots of features to make learning each topic lively and memorable.

### Key concepts
Each chapter contains six key concepts and these appear on the opening pages of each chapter; they appear again as you work through the chapter to help you become familiar with them. They are also collected in the back of the book, in a Key concept glossary.

### Quotations
These are taken from holy books. Using them could impress your examiner.

### Activities
The activities reinforce your learning. You can work on them individually or tackle them as a class.

## 4.7 Muslim attitudes to justice and punishment

In this topic you will look at Muslim beliefs about justice, punishment and the death penalty.

**KEY CONCEPTS**

**duty** something you do because it is the accepted pattern of behaviour

العدل

*One of the 99 names of Allah is Al-Hakam, which means 'The Just'. This teaches Muslims how important justice is.*

### Allah is just
Justice is extremely important to Muslims because they believe that Allah is just. He created everybody equal and treats his creation with justice and fairness. Allah expects everybody to treat each other in the same way.

Those who do not treat other people with justice will be judged accordingly when they go before Allah on the Day of Judgement. If they have not shown mercy to others, they cannot expect Allah to show mercy to them. On the Day of Judgement, the good will be rewarded and the evil punished; that is the justice of Allah.

Muslims believe they have a **duty** to work towards a just society and the Qur'an gives them guidance.

**Activity 1**
Rephrase the quotation from the Qur'an in your own words. What does it teach Muslims about justice?

*Those who seek to redress their wrongs incur no guilt. But great is the guilt of those who oppress their fellow men and conduct themselves with wickedness and injustice in the land. Woeful punishment awaits them.* **(Qur'an 42:40)**

**Useful specialist language**
**Shari'ah law** a code of law based on the teachings of the Qur'an and the practice of the prophet Muhammad

### Shari'ah law
Muslims are taught that it is Allah's will that they should follow the straight path of life set out in the Qur'an. The Islamic legal system is called **Shari'ah law**. It is based on the idea of justice for everyone and it puts the teachings of the Qur'an into laws. All Muslims are entitled to equal treatment under Shari'ah law. Islamic courts use Shari'ah law to decide on just punishments if the laws of Allah are broken.

**Activity 2**
Try this (c) question:

*The death penalty is a just punishment for murder.*

Give **two** reasons why a religious believer might agree or disagree with this statement. (4)

### Justice is most important
Islam is a religion that is based on peace and justice. For some crimes, Muslims believe that death is a just punishment. To let someone off would be an injustice for the victim and their family, it would also be damaging to society. Although society must punish a criminal for their behaviour, Muslims believe that Allah will be the ultimate judge and he will punish them in the afterlife.

Islam regards the death penalty as the correct form of retribution for some crimes. Capital punishment is also regarded as a deterrent and a punishment that safeguards people's lives and property.

Capital punishment can only be legal if the accused is given a fair trial in a court of law and found guilty. Other less severe punishments are also possible under Shari'ah law and these must be weighed up against the crime. However, in the most severe cases, capital punishment is believed to be the just punishment.

*Islam permits the death penalty to be carried out by firing squad, beheading, hanging or stoning.*

*... whoever killed a human being, except as punishment for murder or other villainy in the land, shall be regarded as having killed all mankind; and that whoever saved a human life shall be regarded as having saved all mankind.* **(Qur'an 5:32)**

*... you shall not kill – for that is forbidden by God – except for a just cause.* **(Qur'an 6:151)**

Shari'ah law permits the death penalty for:
- **deliberate murder**. The family of a victim has the right to say whether or not they wish the murderer to be executed.
- **threatening to undermine the authority**. This is a wide area, which is interpreted in different ways that range from treason and terrorism to adultery and homosexuality. It also permits the death penalty for a Muslim who rejects their religion and actively works against it.

### Not all Muslims demand the death penalty
Some Muslims point out that the Qur'an does permit other punishments. For instance, the family of a victim is permitted to pardon the criminal and accept a payment of 'blood money' rather than insist on execution. Whilst all Muslim countries have the death penalty on their statute books, some countries have not used it for many years.

**Activity 3**
For discussion: Is it a good idea to let a victim's family decide on the right punishment? Why? Note down the points given for and against this.

**☑ Check you have learnt:**
- why justice is important to Muslims
- why most Muslims accept the need for capital punishment
- why some Muslims do not agree with capital punishment.

**TRY YOUR SKILL AT THIS**
**The (d) question:**
Explain from **two** different traditions the teachings about capital punishment. (You must state the religious traditions you are referring to.) (6)
**Hint:** Use these pages along with pages 110–111 to answer from the Christian and Muslim traditions.

### Useful specialist language
You will not be asked to give the meaning of these words, but you can boost your marks by using them correctly in your exam answers.

### Statements
These statements in speech bubbles are practice for the (c) question in the exam.

### Check you have learnt
This asks you to summarize what you have learnt about each topic, so you can check you've grasped the key points.

### Try your skill at this
These questions will give you an opportunity to practise your newly-learnt skills with exam-style questions, building up your knowledge and confidence.

## Giving you plenty of coaching

In order to help you get the best possible grades that you can, there is plenty of help with improving your exam skills. Within every chapter of study there are three Skills coaching spreads. These are designed to help you become familiar with the five different types of questions you will see on the exam paper.

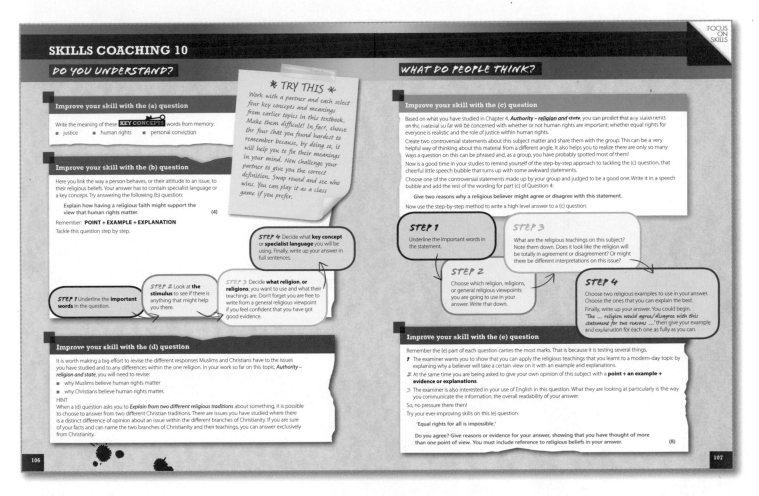

The left-hand page is called 'Do you understand?' because it concentrates on the three questions that test your knowledge and understanding of what you have learnt. This skill carries half the marks.

The right-hand page is called 'What do people think?' because it is asking you to give the different opinions people might have about a statement. Sometimes the opinions that are being asked for are your own. The two questions that are asking this carry half the marks on the paper.

There will be analysis of the questions so you get used to understanding exactly what the examiner is looking for. You will also look closely at the way the examiner marks each type of question with examples of the marking grids that are used. For each type of question you will get step-by-step help with constructing an answer, plus a few chances to 'Be the examiner' yourself. On these occasions you will be reading someone else's answer, comparing it with the marking criteria, and then awarding a grade and giving the student a few tips on improving their marks!

Each End of chapter check reminds you of what you should have learnt in that chapter and contains a practice question for you to try out.

Please note that Muslims add the initials *pbuh* (meaning 'peace be upon him') after the prophet Muhammad's name as a sign of respect. In this textbook these initials have been mentioned in the first instance only.

*This is a very exciting course of study with plenty of material to grab your attention and get you arguing. Enjoy!*

# CHAPTER 1    Religion and conflict

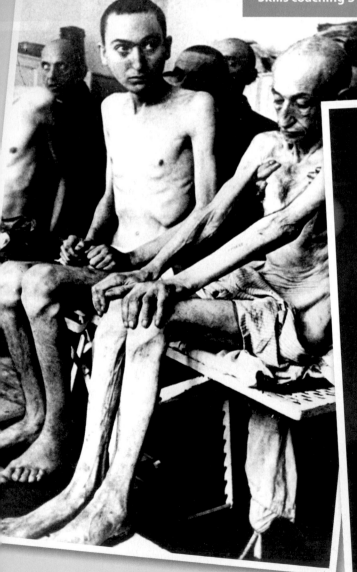

**KEY CONCEPTS** KEY C

**conflict** clashes and breakdowns of relationships

**interfaith dialogue** exploring common grounds between different faith groups

**just war** a war undertaken to protect the innocent or those being violated and to restore justice and peace

**non-violent protest** showing disapproval without damaging property or causing any threat

**pacifism** the belief that any form of violence or war is unacceptable

**reconciliation** bringing harmony to a situation of disagreement and discord

In this topic you will examine some of the reasons people give for the existence of suffering.

### Useful specialist language

**moral evil** suffering caused by humans

**natural evil** disasters and suffering that happen in the natural world

*Unexpected floods have ruined these people's homes.*

### Activity 1

Look at these pictures and decide:

a) who is suffering?

b) who caused it?

c) was it deserved?

*This baby was born with severe abnormalities.*

## Suffering is a problem

It is hard to understand why bad things happen to people and why they suffer when they don't seem to deserve it. As you have probably worked out from the pictures, there can be many reasons for suffering. Humans may be responsible for some of the suffering, but what about the rest? Suffering is often thought of as a form of evil.

### Moral evil

*Moral evil* is when suffering is caused by people. It is often a case of someone deliberately hurting another, perhaps by hitting them. Moral evil can also be accidental. The child who deliberately plays with fireworks after they have been warned of the dangers and then suffers facial injuries is a victim of moral evil, even though the injury was self-inflicted. Consider the case of the long-distance truck driver who falls asleep at the wheel and then crashes into the car in front, killing a young family. He never intended that horror, but he was responsible for the suffering.

### Natural evil

At other times disaster strikes, like an earthquake, and causes suffering on a huge scale. When a natural disaster happens, like the Boxing Day Tsunami of 2004, it is hard to know who is to blame for it. Around 300,000 innocent people were killed but nobody was responsible. It was just a freak of nature and is considered a *natural evil*.

War has forced these refugees to flee their homes.

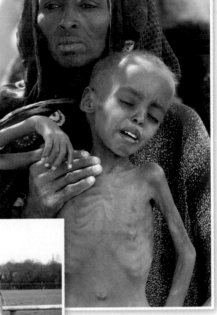

This family in the developing world is starving.

There are charities who rescue abused animals.

## It's fate

Not everybody looks for a religious reason for suffering; some say it's just fate. It's bad luck if you find yourself in the wrong place at the wrong time, but there is nothing you can do about it.

## Why do the innocent suffer?

The picture of the baby suffering raises many questions. Is it an example of moral evil or natural evil? It is certainly possible to make an argument for both. Everybody agrees it is bad and most find it hard to understand why the innocent suffer. Some look to religion for answers.

### Activity 2

For discussion: Insurance companies call an accident that occurs as a result of natural evil, like death or injury from a lightning strike, 'an act of God' and do not normally pay compensation for it. Why do you think they use this term? Would you say it was an accurate title? Why?

### Activity 3

People who suffer usually deserve it.

Do you agree? Give **two** reasons for your opinion.

### ✓ Check you have learnt:

- how suffering can be caused by natural disasters
- two different ways people might cause suffering
- the difference between moral evil and natural evil.

### TRY YOUR SKILL AT THIS

Explain some of the reasons why people suffer.

Most Christians accept that it is very sad when people suffer and they do their best to help those who are suffering. Where Christians differ from non-religious people is in the reasons why they think suffering exists.

## Nobody said it had to be easy!

For some Christians, evil and suffering are life's tests. The way we react to people who need our help determines what will happen to us in the afterlife. Some Christians think that God decides whether a person will go to heaven or hell on the basis of how they behave towards those who suffer. Others believe that suffering has a different purpose; it is there to strengthen a person's character and make them a better individual.

## We aren't robots

We certainly aren't programmed like a computer. We have the freedom to choose how we want to react to any situation. This means people are free to do good or bad. Christians believe that God deliberately created people with free will. Therefore, if a person hurts another, it is the fault of the human who chooses to make someone suffer, not God.

## You are only human

Another thing Christians say is that no one can expect to understand why suffering happens as we're only human. How can we understand the mind of God the creator? Our intelligence is minuscule compared to God's. God will have reasons for permitting suffering in the world, but it is extremely unlikely that humans will be able to understand those reasons. The Book of Job in the Old Testament is about a holy man who undergoes the most terrible suffering for no apparent reason. The lesson Job has to learn is that he must accept that God is in control and God has reasons for what is happening, even though Job can't understand them.

### Activity 1

> Suffering should be accepted as a normal part of life.

Give **two** reasons why a religious believer might agree or disagree with this statement.

*People have free will to choose how they behave. This robot can't. His behaviour is determined by his program.*

*This is one reason why some Christians believe there is suffering in the world.*

## Activity 2

Write a longer caption for the Garden of Eden picture explaining why some Christians think this story holds the key to human suffering. Is this a good explanation for the scenes of suffering shown on pages 10–11? Why?

## Activity 3

Draw a spider diagram with JESUS in the centre. Use it to show how Jesus affects the attitude of some Christians towards suffering.

## The example of Jesus

When Jesus lived on earth as a man he endured terrible suffering, even though, as the Son of God, he was perfect. Jesus' suffering had a purpose because it gave people everlasting life.

## Suffering is a punishment

Some Christians believe that the Adam and Eve story holds the answer, because it says God created the first two humans with free will. Adam and Eve used their free will to disobey God who punished them for choosing evil and sent them out of the Garden of Eden. For some Christians, suffering is a punishment sent by God to make people repent their evil ways and turn back to God.

## Responding through worship

For some Christians, their response to suffering is to turn to God in prayer to ask him to ease people's suffering. Some turn to their scriptures for understanding and guidance on what God wants them to do. Others meet in groups to hold healing services where their worship focuses on the needs of those who are suffering.

## Don't just sit there, do something!

Most Christians don't sit around trying to understand why suffering happens because Jesus taught them that the correct response to suffering is to help people. Help can take many forms, from dropping coins in a collecting tin to joining with a community to do something practical to help those in need.

**✓ Check you have learnt:**

- three different Christian responses to suffering
- what Jesus taught Christians about suffering
- the connection between free will and suffering.

**TRY YOUR SKILL AT THIS**

Explain **two** different reasons a religious believer might give for the existence of suffering.

**In this topic you will consider how some Muslims respond to suffering.**

### It is part of Allah's plan

Muslims believe that Allah has a plan for everyone and suffering may be part of that plan. It is not for us to question what Allah intends, nor to try to understand Allah's reasons. His intelligence is far greater than the humans he created, so we stand no chance of understanding the mind of Allah. What Muslims are sure of is that no one is ever given more suffering than they can cope with.

### Suffering is a test

The Qur'an teaches Muslims that they should accept suffering as a test set by Allah. On the Day of Judgement, they will go before Allah and be judged on the way they reacted to their own suffering or the suffering of others. If they accepted their own suffering as being the will of Allah and did not become bitter or complain, then they will be rewarded in the afterlife. If they reacted with love and compassion to those who were suffering around them, that too will be rewarded.

Muslims believe that Allah created everyone with free will and wants his people to choose to submit to the will of Allah. Free will means people have a choice. Some will reject the way of Allah and choose evil. Following the way of Shaitan (Satan) may lead to suffering in this life, but will certainly lead to punishment in the afterlife where a person will have to pay for their wrongdoing.

### Suffering brings a person closer to Allah

The way a person deals with their own suffering on earth can be a test of their faith in Allah. Those who approach suffering with a calm acceptance, understanding it is part of Allah's plan, will find their faith in Allah strengthened.

*One of the 99 names of Allah is Ar-Rahim, the compassionate. Muslims believe that there is always a reason for suffering and Allah ensures no one has more suffering than they can bear.*

### Activity 1

> Suffering is there for a reason.

Give **two** reasons why a religious believer might agree or disagree with this statement.

### Activity 2

Role play a conversation between Asma, a young Muslim student who calmly accepts her disability, and her friend Vikki who cannot understand Asma's attitude.

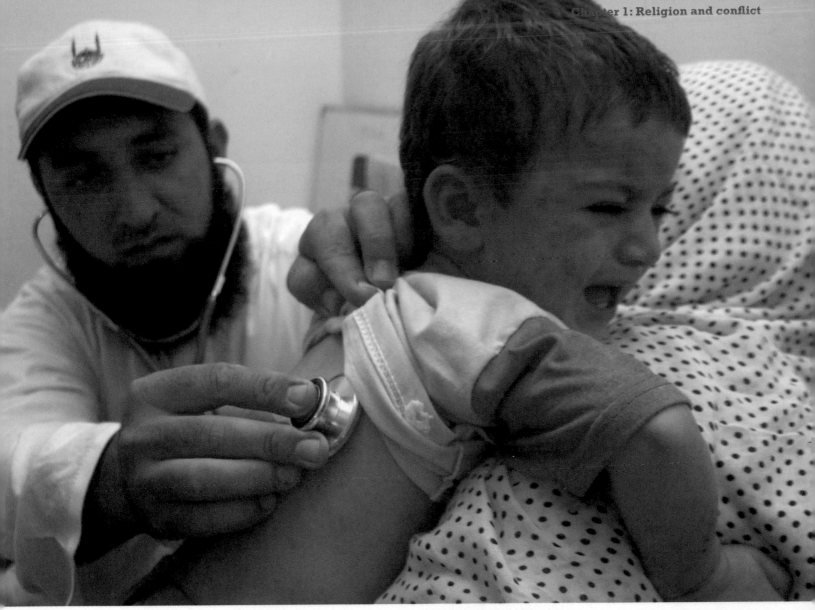

*This doctor is caring for a victim of the fighting on the North West Frontier Province of Pakistan. Islamic Relief set up Mercy Centres in the area to provide healthcare, trauma recovery and other facilities for the three million people forced to flee the conflict in 2009.*

# Helping to relieve suffering

Muslims are taught that those who choose to give help to people who are suffering will please Allah and in the afterlife they will draw closer to Allah. The Qur'an teaches that the way in which a Muslim reacts to people who are suffering will be judged by Allah. Muslims have the example set by Prophet Muhammad (pbuh) to give them guidance on how they should live and treat others.

Zakah, the third pillar of Islam, teaches Muslims to give 2.5 per cent of their income to help the poor and needy and relieve their suffering. Some Muslims choose to make other voluntary donations to help the needy. This might be in response to a television appeal for donations following an international disaster, or coins put in the tin of a charity collector outside a supermarket. A few Muslims choose to participate in the work of relief agencies and travel to disaster zones to help relieve suffering.

## Activity 3

Draw a spider diagram to show the different ways in which some Muslims respond to suffering.

## Check you have learnt:

- how suffering might be part of Allah's plan
- how suffering is a test
- the connection between responses to suffering and the afterlife.

## TRY YOUR SKILL AT THIS

Explain some of the reasons why a religious believer might say that good can come out of suffering.

## How do religious believers support those who are suffering?

In this topic you will examine the ways a Christian and a Muslim community help those who are suffering.

### Activity 1

What are **three** different ways shown here in which Christians support people who are suffering? Which do you feel makes the most impact and why?

### Activity 2

> Giving up an hour of your time is hardly likely to change the world.

Give **two** reasons why a religious believer might agree or disagree with this statement.

# St Stephen's Church noticeboard

## NEED HELP WITH A HANDICAPPED CHILD?

Please ask us.

St Stephen's has several schemes to help you.

Saturday afternoon playgroup for mentally and physically handicapped children.

Assistance from a team of trained volunteers, including some sixth formers from the Catholic College.

It is totally paid for by the parish through donations and fundraising activities.

* * *

### SUPPORT GROUP

We also have a monthly support group and special mass for families of handicapped children. You don't have to feel isolated. The parish is here to help you.

Refreshments provided, along with help and support. Social meeting followed by mass with volunteers to help the children join in.

* * *

### NEED JUST A FEW HOURS' BREAK?

Families who have received specialist training will look after your handicapped child so you can take a much needed break from your loving but heavy responsibility.

Father John will give you more details.

### Thank you

to everyone from the church who took part in the sponsored walk in aid of the Hospice last Saturday. We raised £516, which joins the money raised from the carol singing at the supermarket before Christmas. A cheque will be presented to the Thames-Side Hospice next month.

### DONATIONS OF TOILETRIES

are requested to make up small packages of essential requirements for the homeless. Please leave donations on the bench inside the church porch or put them in the collecting box in the Spar supermarket. Thank you.

Door-to-door collectors required for the **Poppy Day Appeal** in aid of wounded servicemen and their families. If you can spare an hour or two to help, please tell the Reverend Judy.

# Central Mosque noticeboard

Thanks to everyone who gave up their Saturday to help at Islamic Relief's clothes recycling depot. Last year, the charity raised £270,000 from all the clothes donated and used the money on projects to help the needy. Keep the clothes coming in! Nothing is wasted. They are carefully sorted and appropriate ones are sent to disaster areas around the world. The rest are sold in our charity shops to raise money to relieve suffering.

And don't forget that recycling is good for the environment too!

## SPONSOR AN ORPHAN

By pledging £27 a month, you can make sure that one child will get a good level of care and education. Your sponsorship will pay for that child's:

- school fees
- clothing and footwear
- books and stationery
- travel costs.

The money will also:

- provide for the orphan's family
- pay the cost of a Muslim Hands worker to check on the orphan's well-being.

Go to our website www.muslimhands.org for more details of how you can relieve a child's suffering.

## BECOME A VOLUNTEER

*Can you spread the word?*

### Create a buzz about Muslim Aid in your area

You know your friends, right? There's the loud one, the funny one, the shy one? Well, that's what it's like to volunteer for Muslim Aid, except it's more like a family – a big mix of personalities from all backgrounds and communities – with one aim: to serve humanity and to help our brothers and sisters escape a life of poverty across the world.

### Could you help us?

- Are you aged between 16 and 60?
- Are you passionate about tackling global poverty?
- Are you based in Birmingham, Nottingham, Sheffield, Bradford, Leeds, Manchester, Leicester or Luton?
- Could you help us with mosque collections in Ramadan, street collections, fundraising events and other activities?

*If yes, get in touch with us at Muslim Aid www.muslimaid.org.*

## Activity 3

Explain why a Muslim might want to get involved in one of these activities.

### ✔ Check you have learnt:

- two practical ways in which Christians can help to relieve suffering
- two practical ways in which Muslims can help to relieve suffering.

### TRY YOUR SKILL AT THIS

Explain from **two** religious traditions how believers might take practical action to relieve suffering.

## DO YOU UNDERSTAND?

**Half of the marks on this paper will be given for your understanding of the topics. These questions all begin with the word _Explain_. What the examiner is asking you to do is to describe fully what you know about a topic. This may include giving an example and explaining it.**

### The (a) question

This is the simplest of the explain questions and is worth 2 marks. The examiner is asking for the meaning of some of the key concepts in a topic. The key concepts in the topic **Religion and Conflict** are on page 9.

So far no key concepts have appeared. However, some useful specialist language has been used. Look back at these on page 10 and familiarize yourself with the terms and their meanings.

### The (b) question

This question asks you to apply your knowledge to one or more of the religions you have studied. This question always starts: _Explain how having a religious faith might ..._ . The examiner is asking you to look at the way a religious person behaves and to suggest the reasons for this. This question is worth 4 marks.

Here is a typical (b) question based on the material you have studied so far:

> **Explain how having a religious faith might influence a person's attitude towards suffering. (4)**

If you were going to tackle this question you could choose to answer it with a Christian in mind, a Muslim in mind, or by referring to both of them. Make sure you tell the examiner which religion you are talking about.

Other (b) questions might ask you to:

> **Explain how having a religious faith might encourage a person to accept their suffering.   (4)**

> **Explain how having a religious faith might lead a person to help those who are suffering.   (4)**

Choose one of these three (b) questions and write your answer.

### The (d) question

This question is testing your understanding of how two religions, or two religious traditions, view the same issue. This question is worth 6 marks.

The two religions you have studied in this book are Christianity and Islam so you could answer from each of those. It is also possible to answer totally from Christianity if you know that there are two traditions within Christianity that hold opposing views. For example, you might write about the Quaker attitude and the Catholic attitude towards the same issue if you know their views are very different.

A good way to start your part (i) answer is _Some Christians think ..._ and your part (ii) answer _Some Muslims think ..._ . Of course you can write about them in the opposite order, no problem, but make sure you always begin your answer with the name of the religious tradition you are writing about.

Here are some typical (d) questions:

> **Explain from two different religious traditions the attitude of believers towards suffering.   (6)**

> **Explain from two different religious traditions how believers may help people who are suffering.   (6)**

**Tip:**
In your answer always write '_Some Christians_' or '_Some Muslims_' or you could say '_Many Christians_' or '_Many Muslims_'. This is because everybody is an individual even if they do belong to the same religion. It is quite possible that some members of that religion hold slightly different views to others, so play safe!

# WHAT DO PEOPLE THINK?

The (c) and (e) questions are very similar. Both are asking you to give people's opinions about a statement.

## The (c) question

The (c) question usually starts with a statement in a speech bubble. The (c) question is asking you to use the religious teachings you have learnt about an issue and apply them to a real situation.

Under the speech bubble, the (c) question will always ask you to:

**Give two reasons why a religious believer might agree or disagree with this statement.**

You can earn 4 marks for your answer.

You do not have to give both reasons from the same religion, but you can if you wish. It is also possible to answer this from a general religious point of view, without mentioning a specific religion, if you are confident that you have the evidence.

Here are some typical (c) questions:

> **People suffer for a purpose.**

> **People are the cause of suffering, not God.**

**Give two reasons why a religious believer might agree or disagree with this statement.** (4)

**Tip:**
Remember that some believers in the same religion don't always share the same views, so you could say *'Some believers would agree because ...'* and *'Other believers would disagree because ...'*.

## The (e) question

The (e) question carries 8 marks. This time you are being asked for your opinion. To convince the examiner that you have really given some consideration to the topic, you are asked to back up your view with reasons or evidence. This is a Religious Studies paper, so it is not surprising that you are also asked to refer to the views of a religion. Don't be afraid to disagree with what that religion says if you want to. That is perfectly acceptable as long as you give your reasons. In Topic 1, the (e) question carries an extra 5 marks for spelling, punctuation and the accurate use of grammar.

Here are some typical (e) questions:

> **'Religion is the cause of most of the suffering in the world.'**

**Do you agree? Give reasons or evidence for your answer, showing that you have thought of more than one point of view. You must include reference to religious beliefs in your answer.** (8 + 5)

> **'If someone is suffering, it is probably their own fault.'**

**Do you agree? Give reasons or evidence for your answer, showing that you have thought of more than one point of view. You must include reference to religious beliefs in your answer.** (8 + 5)

## What do Christians think about war?

In this topic you will examine some of the Christian attitudes to war.

**KEY CONCEPTS** KEY C

**just war** a war undertaken to protect the innocent or those being violated and to restore justice and peace

## Activity 1

Try this (c) question:

> War is evil.

Give **two** reasons why a religious believer might agree or disagree with this statement. (4)

## War is a difficult issue

Because war involves violence and killing, Christians, like many non-religious people, find it difficult to decide whether or not it is justified. Most Christians accept that war may be a necessary evil. Although they would prefer everyone to live in peace, Christians understand that sometimes fighting is the only way to overcome evil. Scenes like those that showed the liberation of people from the death camp at Auschwitz convinced many Christians that World War II was justified because it ended the atrocities suffered by Jews and others at the hands of the Nazis.

## What does the Bible teach about war?

In the Old Testament there are many examples of God's chosen people going to war and stories in the New Testament show that Jesus lived in a country under military occupation. Jesus never condemned the soldiers; indeed, in Luke 7:1–10, he praised a Roman soldier for his faith. Jesus also told his followers that they should pay the correct taxes to the Roman authorities. This leads Christians to understand that they must always obey the orders of the state, which might include going to war.

In a radio broadcast before he became Pope Benedict XVI, Cardinal Joseph Ratzinger said that he believed that Christians could not ignore evil aggression that threatened to destroy, not only Christian values, but that would kill large numbers of people, and even destroy humanity. Ratzinger stated that people had a duty to defend themselves and others: if a father sees his family being attacked, it is his duty to defend them in every possible way, including using the same amount of violence as the attacker.

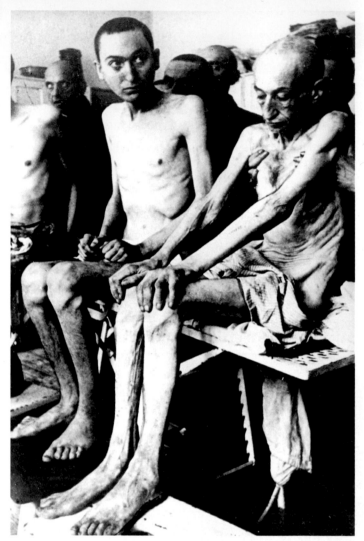

*Scenes like this, the liberation of people from the death camp at Auschwitz at the end of World War II, convince most Christians that sometimes war may be the only way to defeat evil.*

## Activity 2

What reasons does the Pope give for permitting war? Would you agree with him? Why?

# A just war

Many Christians and others believe that, no matter how desirable peace is, there may be very good reasons why it is necessary to go to war in some situations. Refusing to fight could allow evil to win. Over the centuries, Christian philosophers have worked at drawing up rules to define when it is right to go to war and the fairest way to conduct a war. These rules are for a **just war** and remain the basis of the rules used by the West today.

### The theory of a just war

1  **The war must be for a just cause**. This includes resisting aggression, or for self-defence or fighting to remove an injustice.

2  **A war must be declared by a lawful authority**. A war can only be declared by a government, a ruler or the UN, but never by a private citizen.

3  **A war must only be fought to bring about good**. This means that a war can be fought to restore peace, or to prevent further suffering or any other form of evil. Once that end has been achieved, fighting must stop.

4  **War must be a last resort**. All other peaceful ways of resolving the problem, such as negotiations, must be tried first.

5  **There must be a reasonable chance of success**. This means that no country is to go to war when they stand no chance of winning. This is to prevent lives being lost unnecessarily.

6  **Only necessary force must be used to achieve the aim**. This means that it would be totally unjustified to use nuclear weapons against a small country over something like a boundary dispute. The clause is intended to prevent one country taking the opportunity of a war to totally annihilate the other.

7  **Only legitimate targets should be attacked**. These would be military installations and other soldiers. Hospitals, homes and civilians are not to be attacked.

*The widespread destruction caused by a nuclear bomb has made many people question whether weapons of mass destruction can ever be justified.*

## Activity 3

For discussion:

a) In 1963, Pope John XXIII said: "It is impossible to conceive of a just war in a nuclear age." Do you agree?

b) Read the theory of a just war. Are there any rules that would be broken if weapons of mass destruction were used?

✓ **Check you have learnt:**

- what is meant by a just war
- two reasons why Christians might accept war.

**TRY YOUR SKILL AT THIS**

**The (b) question:**

Explain how having a religious faith might lead some religious believers to say war may be acceptable. (4)

# 1.6 Why are some people pacifists?

In this topic you will learn about the reasons why some people believe that war is never acceptable and how they make use of methods of non-violent protest to make their views known.

## KEY CONCEPTS KEY

**conflict** clashes and breakdowns of relationships

**non-violent protest** showing disapproval without damaging property or causing any threat

**pacifism** the belief that any form of violence or war is unacceptable

## Violence solves nothing

Some people believe that war does more harm than good. They point out that, despite the so-called 'surgical precision' of modern weapons, 90 per cent of casualties in today's wars are innocent civilians. Land is ruined by war for years afterwards and the huge sums of money spent on war would be better spent on saving lives and preventing suffering.

Some religious believers think war is wrong because they believe we are all God's creatures and we all have a right to life. Many religious and non-religious people agree that war is wrong because it causes innocent people to suffer.

Although Roman Catholics are not necessarily against war, the Catholic Association for Overseas Development (CAFOD) states:

"War and conflict have a direct impact on development. In times of war crops are destroyed, or people may be forced to leave their homes before they can plant or harvest crops. Millions of people flee areas where there is fighting to look for safety. Anti-personnel landmines make land unusable. Roads and bridges are destroyed, schools and health clinics closed."

### Activity 1

List the problems CAFOD state are caused by war. Rank them in the order of suffering caused, starting with the most serious down to the least important.

### Activity 2

Try this (c) question:

> Modern warfare is an efficient way to solve a dispute quickly.

Give **two** reasons why a religious believer might agree or disagree with this statement. (4)

STOP THE WAR · NOT IN MY NAME · DON'T ATTACK IRAQ · NO WAR ON IRAQ · STOP THE WAR · Freedom For Palestine · NO WAR ON IRAQ · STOP THE WAR

STOP THE WAR

*Around three-quarters of a million people marched through London in 2003 in a non-violent protest about going to war against Iraq. Clearly, peace is an issue that concerns religious and non-religious people alike.*

## Pacifists

People who do not accept **conflict** as the solution to any dispute are called pacifists. Some pacifists are religious, many are not. All believe that there are better ways of solving disputes than going to war. Some use methods of **non-violent protest** to draw attention to their message. This might include campaigning, joining public marches, taking part in a sit-in, or some other event that causes sufficient disruption for people to take notice but does no harm.

Many Christians support peace, but only a few are pacifists who totally reject war. Those Christians point out that Jesus preached love and peace. He said:

> *Do not take revenge on someone who wrongs you. If anyone slaps you on the right cheek, let him slap your left cheek too.* (Matthew 5:39)

Quakers are the only Christian group totally committed to **pacifism**. They say violence is always destructive and can never achieve any lasting peace. Instead, Quakers work to tackle the cause of conflicts and try to arrange peace negotiations.

They say:

"… [O]ur conviction [is] that love is at the heart of existence and all human beings are equal in the eyes of God, and that we must live in a way that reflects this. It has led Quakers to refuse military service, and to become involved in a wide range of peace activities from practical work in areas affected by violent conflict to the development of alternatives to violence at all levels from personal to international."

*Some Quakers joined peace activists in a year-long blockade of the Faslane nuclear weapons base in Scotland as a non-violent protest against Britain's Trident nuclear weapons system. You can read more about this on page 120.*

### Check you have learnt:

- why some people are pacifists
- what is meant by non-violent protest
- three forms of non-violent protest.

### TRY YOUR SKILL AT THIS

**The (e) question:**

'Non-violent protests don't achieve anything.'

Do you agree? Give reasons or evidence for your answer, showing that you have thought of more than one point of view. You must include reference to religious beliefs in your answer. (8 + 5)

## Activity 3

Debate whether war is always wrong, taking into consideration the following pieces of information:

- For the cost of one jet-fighter plane, three million children could be vaccinated against disease.
- Disease kills more people than war. World War I killed nine million people, but over 20 million died from the flu in 1918.

## Activity 4

Find out more about Bruce Kent, who is seen wearing black in the picture above. Then give a presentation explaining why this Roman Catholic priest controversially became a nuclear disarmament campaigner.

## DO YOU UNDERSTAND?

### The (a) question

So far in your study of Christian attitudes towards war you have met the **KEY CONCEPTS**:

- just war
- pacifism
- conflict
- non-violent protest

It is worth bearing in mind that there have been other important concepts that you could be asked about. Try learning the definition of each key concept when it appears on the page.

> This is how the examiner looks at your answer:
>
> | A very brief explanation. | 1 mark |
> |---|---|
> | A fully developed explanation. | 2 marks |

### The (b) question

This is the question that asks you to link what a religion teaches with how a person might behave or think. It's worth 4 marks and those marks are for making that link.

| Level 1 | • One basic point linking beliefs and action. | 1 mark |
|---|---|---|
| Level 2 | • One basic point + example. | 2 marks |
| Level 3 | • One basic point + example + explanation or evidence. | 3 marks |
| Level 4 | • Two basic points + examples.<br>• One basic point + example + well-developed explanation. | 4 marks |

Here is a typical (b) question:

> Explain how having a religious faith might influence a person's attitude to war. (4)

Look carefully at what is required to get 4 marks and aim for that in your answer.

> **Tip:**
> The examiner is looking for good use of religious language in your answers, so take every opportunity to include it and possibly some specialist language. Without any specialist language, you are unlikely to move above Level 1.

### The (d) question

Here, you are asked for your understanding of the way two religious traditions approach the same issue. It might be:

> Explain from two religious traditions attitudes towards non-violent protest. (6)

This is how the examiner will be looking to reward your (d) answer:

| Level 1 | • One basic statement. | 1 mark |
|---|---|---|
| Level 2 | • One basic statement + development. | 2 marks |
| Level 3 | • One basic statement + two examples. | 3/4 marks |
| Level 4 | NB: To get to this level you must have written about both religions.<br>• One basic statement + two examples and one basic statement + development.<br>• One basic statement + two examples and another basic statement + two examples. | 5/6 marks |

> **Tip:**
> The more evidence you include in your answer, the more opportunity you are giving the examiner to award you full marks.

Write an answer to the (d) question above. Then swap answers with a partner and use the mark scheme to award a mark and a level for each other's answers. Tell them what you think they would have scored and why.

# WHAT DO PEOPLE THINK?

## The (c) question

This question is asking you to decide how a religious believer might react to a statement. You can answer from a religion of your choice or a general religious viewpoint.

It is also worth remembering that religious believers may well share the same views as people who belong to no religion. This is no problem provided you explain why these beliefs matter to a religious believer. For instance, most people think peace is important, but a Christian believer might explain that living in a peaceful manner is what God intends humanity to do.

> Pacifism is a waste of time.

**Give two reasons why a religious believer might agree or disagree with this statement. (4)**

Here is how the examiner will be looking to reward your (c) answer:

| Level 1 | ● One point + example. | 1 mark |
|---|---|---|
| Level 2 | ● One point + example + explanation (or evidence).<br>● One point + example and another point + example. | 2 marks |
| Level 3 | ● One point + example + explanation and another point + example. | 3 marks |
| Level 4 | ● One point + example + explanation and another point + example + explanation. | 4 marks |

Answer the (c) question above and aim for a Level 4 answer.

**Tip:**
The question does say agree or disagree. You are perfectly free to mix and match your answer. You could give one reason why a religious believer would agree with the statement and one reason why a religious believer (from the same or a different religion) would disagree. It is the evidence you give that will gain the marks.

## The (e) question

This question asks what a religious believer thinks about an issue and also what you think. Here is a typical (e) question:

'War doesn't achieve anything.'

Do you agree? Give reasons or evidence for your answer, showing that you have thought of more than one point of view. You must include reference to a religious belief in your answer. (8 + 5)

This is how the examiner is looking to reward your answer:

| Level 1 | ● One simple point + example.<br>● One simple point + two examples. | 1 mark<br>2 marks | +5 marks in Topic 1 for spelling, punctuaton and grammar |
|---|---|---|---|
| Level 2 | ● One point + example + explanation.<br>● One point + example + explanation with religious example. | 3 marks<br>4 marks | |
| Level 3 | ● One point + religious examples + explanations and an alternative viewpoint. | 5/6 marks | |
| Level 4 | ● Two well-argued views that each contain one point + example + explanation + religious evidence. | 7/8 marks | |

The (e) question also carries the **Q**uality of **W**ritten **C**ommunication (QWC), which means your marks for this question will be affected by the quality of your English. This will be particularly noticeable in Levels 3 and 4 where good written English will help you achieve the higher of the two marks. Remember, in Topic 1 the (e) question carries 5 extra marks for spelling, punctuation and the accurate use of grammar.

Answer the (e) question. Then compare your answer with the mark scheme. What could you have done to improve your mark?

**In this topic you will study Muslim attitudes to war.**

### Useful specialist language

**jihad** means to strive

**a greater jihad** is the struggle within a person to resist temptation and do good rather than evil

**a lesser jihad** is a military struggle to defend Islam

Although Islam is a religion of peace, Muslims do not believe in pacifism. The Qur'an teaches that sometimes war is necessary to conquer evil but, once evil has been defeated, fighting must stop and peace be restored.

## Jihad

A Muslim's life is directed towards pleasing Allah, and this involves getting rid of evil and establishing a peaceful society on earth. The struggle against evil is called **jihad**, but the Qur'an teaches Muslims that the struggle against evil must first start within themselves.

A **greater jihad** is the personal battle that everyone has with themselves, whether to do what is right or succumb to temptation and do what we know is wrong.

Muslims also understand that, on occasions, it may be necessary to fight against evil in the world. Taking military action in order to bring about a just society is a **lesser jihad** and Muslims should go to war if that is necessary. They must also fight to preserve Islam if the religion comes under attack.

## The rules of warfare

Muslims also have rules about how war (a lesser jihad) should be conducted. These rules are similar to those for a just war, but the conflict is sometimes referred to as a holy war.

*Many Muslims thought that the invasion of Iraq by the USA and the UK was unjust. They joined non-Muslims in staging peaceful protests in London and elsewhere around the world.*

- **War must be a last resort**, which means that every effort should be made to solve the dispute by non-violent means.

- **A war can only be started and controlled by a religious leader** but Islam teaches Muslims that they must not be the first to declare war.

- **War must have a just cause**, which might be self-defence to prevent people suffering injustice or to protect the religion from attack.

- **The aim of a war must be to bring about good.** Muslims are taught that it is wrong to fight as an act of aggression or to conquer another country. The aim has to be to bring about a just society.

- **Killing must not be indiscriminate, innocent civilians should not suffer** – particularly women, children and the elderly.

- **Once the aim has been achieved, fighting must stop, mercy be shown and peace restored.**

In addition to these rules, there are many others about the conduct of a holy war, such as treating wounded enemies in exactly the same way as Muslims treat their own wounded. The women and children of the enemy side must not be harmed; neither should any trees, crops or animals. Enemies should be offered the chance to convert to Islam. Prophet Muhammad was himself involved in fighting wars to establish peace, and Muslims look to his teachings and his example when deciding the right conduct of war.

## Guidance from the Qur'an

 *If they incline to peace, make peace with them, and put your trust in God. It is surely He who hears all and knows all.* (Qur'an 8:61)

*Paradise [is for those] who curb their anger and forgive their fellow men.* (Qur'an 3:134)

*Good deeds and evil deeds are not equal. Requite evil with good, and he who is your enemy will become your dearest friend.* (Qur'an 41:34)

*Fight for the sake of God those that fight against you, but do not attack them first.* (Qur'an 2:190)

*There shall be no compulsion in religion.* (Qur'an 2:256)

## The obligation to fight

The Qur'an and the teachings of Muhammad tell Muslims that if all these criteria are fulfilled, it is their religious duty to go to war. Any Muslim killed whilst fighting the jihad will go directly to paradise.

*Muslims must fight if their religion is being threatened.*

**Activity 1**

List the points these quotations from the Qur'an teach Muslims about the conduct of a holy war.

**Activity 2**

Try this (c) question:

> Nuclear war can never be justified.

Give **two** reasons why a religious believer might agree or disagree with this statement. (4)

**Activity 3**

Explain why some Muslims might say that tabloid newspapers misrepresent the concept of jihad.

**Check you have learnt:**

- the meaning of jihad, a lesser and a greater jihad
- four points necessary for a holy war
- the Muslim attitude to peace.

**TRY YOUR SKILL AT THIS**

**The (d) question:**

Explain from **two** different religious traditions why many believers would say that terrorism is not acceptable. (You must state the religious traditions you are referring to.) (6)

## Peace and reconciliation

**In this topic you will examine issues of peace and reconciliation.**

**reconciliation** bringing harmony to a situation of disagreement and discord

**interfaith dialogue** exploring common ground between different faith groups

## Activity 1

Design a flyer for a newly-formed interfaith group stressing the advantages to the whole community of religions getting to know each other better.

Even though many people are convinced war may be the only answer to some disputes, there is widespread agreement that more can be achieved if disputes are settled harmoniously. The ideal is to achieve **reconciliation** between those in conflict. Reconciliation is important, whether it is a small-scale dispute where a couple continually fall out, or whether it is a large-scale dispute where countries are on the brink of armed conflict. What both need is a way forward where differences can be settled, honour satisfied and peace restored. When the disputes are very personal, such as between friends or members of a family, it is essential that apologies are given and accepted. Only then can the rift be healed and people resume their normal life.

Members of some religions devote much time and effort to attempting reconciliation because they know how destructive conflict is. On a personal level, both Muslims and Christians work with families to heal rifts between husband and wife or between parents and children, because they are convinced of the benefits of a happy peaceful family life.

People often say religion is the biggest cause of wars. Maybe that was true in the past, but if you consider some of the wars in the late twentieth century this hasn't necessarily been the case. However, differences of race or religion do cause fear and suspicion in communities, which can flare up into violence. There have been some very successful attempts to create peace and reconciliation in multi-faith communities using **interfaith dialogue**. This is where members from different religions get together to socialize and discuss their different approaches to issues within their community. Through questions and answers, trust is built up and conflict often averted because each understands the other better.

*This statue is called 'Reconciliation' and stands in the ruins of the old part of Coventry Cathedral. An exact copy of the statue was given to the Peace Garden in Hiroshima to mark 50 years since the end of World War II. It is a token of reconciliation with the people of Japan. On the base, it says: 'Both sculptures remind us that in the face of destructive forces, human dignity and love will triumph over disaster and bring nations together in respect and love.'*

# Peace from violence

One group who have been successfully building up an atmosphere of trust and peace through interfaith activities is the St Ethelburga's Centre.

A terrorist bomb destroyed one of London's oldest churches in 1993 but out of the rubble came the idea for a centre for peace-making. St Ethelburga's Centre, which still carries the same name as the bombed church, was officially opened in 2002 by Prince Charles, as a centre for peace and reconciliation. It hosts meetings between different religions to help them understand their differences and explore ways of working together to resolve religious conflicts around the world. The centre holds interfaith discussions and analysis of different scriptures as well as sessions of storytelling and musical or artistic events. The centre also offers specialist guidance for those wanting to work towards building inter-religious relationships.

*The mediaeval church of St Ethelburg's was devastated by an IRA bomb in April 1993.*

*Architects didn't recreate the building exactly as it had been before, but instead created a building that told the story of its destruction and that was suitable for its new use as a centre for reconciliation and peace.*

**Check you have learnt:**

- what reconciliation is
- how interfaith work is important for peace
- what religions can do to help achieve peace and reconciliation.

## Activity 2

Use St Ethelburga's website (www.stethelburgas.org) to find out more about the centre's work, including The Tent. Under the headline *Peace from Violence*, write a newspaper article about the centre's work.

On a larger scale, members of some religious groups work behind the scenes to help settle differences between countries. At an international level, Quakers work with the UN in Geneva and New York to bring reconciliation between warring countries. Because Quakers have no political connections, countries are often prepared to trust them with peace negotiations.

## Activity 3

Try this (c) question:

> Reconciliation is a sign of weakness.

Give **two** reasons why a religious believer might agree or disagree with this statement. (4)

### TRY YOUR SKILL AT THIS

**The (e) question:**

'You can't be a true religious believer if you mix with people of other religions.'

Do you agree? Give reasons or evidence for your answer, showing that you have thought of more than one point of view. You must include reference to religious beliefs in your answer. (8 + 5)

In this topic you will examine what Muslims and Christians think about the importance of forgiveness.

## Activity 1

In pairs, discuss what happens if someone apologizes but the apology is not accepted. Does this mean forgiveness and reconciliation is a two-way process?

## Forgive and move forward

You may have noticed on page 28 that reconciliation has two parts. One involves apologizing and the other involves accepting that apology. Only when forgiveness has been given can people make progress. This is because the damage that has been done must be repaired before anyone can begin to go forward. Forgiveness is at the heart of Christianity and Islam.

*This altar at Coventry Cathedral is made of two charred roof timbers found in the bombed wreckage of the old cathedral the morning after the Blitz. This altar is a powerful symbol of forgiveness, not revenge, which the Cathedral's leader urged on Christians in the aftermath of the German bombing of Coventry, which killed around 500 people and injured far more. The words behind the altar are 'Father Forgive' to remind people of the futility of war.*

## Activity 2

Draw a diagram to show how forgiveness and reconciliation work.

## Forgiveness in Christianity

Jesus practised forgiveness in his own life and death. In his teaching, he stressed how important forgiveness is and that it is a two-way thing. When praying to God, Jesus told his followers to say:

> *Forgive us the wrongs we have done, as we forgive the wrongs that others have done to us.*
> **(Matthew 6:12)**

When the disciple Peter asked Jesus how many times he should forgive somebody who continually hurt him, Peter suggested 'seven times' Jesus replied, 'No, not seven times … but seventy times seven.' (Matthew 18:21–22). Christians think this means you should forgive someone an infinite number of times.

# Forgiveness in Islam

Many passages in the Qur'an teach Muslims that it is important to forgive somebody who has wronged them.

> *Paradise [is for those] who curb their anger and forgive their fellow men.*
> **(Qur'an 3:134)**

> *Good deeds and evil deeds are not equal. Requite evil with good, and he who is your enemy will become your dearest friend.*
> **(Qur'an 41:34)**

Although humans want to be forgiven by people they have wronged, it is the forgiveness of Allah that matters most to Muslims. By asking people's forgiveness for doing wrong and accepting someone's request for forgiveness, Muslims will please Allah.

The life of the prophet Muhammad offers Muslims many examples of how forgiveness and reconciliation worked at a time when blood feuds and vendettas were common. After Muhammad had captured the city of Makkah, its leaders were brought before him and people expected him to demand their execution. Instead, Muhammad said, "You are all free." This shocked his followers but showed how wise Muhammad was because by forgiving his enemies, he turned them into friends and allies. This teaches Muslims that showing mercy and forgiveness is not a sign of weakness.

Muslims are taught to:

- recognize and admit they have made a mistake
- ask for forgiveness from Allah
- ask for forgiveness from the person they have wronged
- try to make up for the wrong they have done someone
- not commit that sin again.

*When Muslims go on hajj, they stand together on Mount Arafat to pray. During this time, they say they are sorry for their sins and ask for Allah's forgiveness.*

**Activity 3**

Muhammad told his followers to "Be forgiving and control yourself in front of provocation". Give an example of a situation where a person might need to put this into practice. Then describe what would have happened if forgiveness wasn't offered.

**Activity 4**

Try this (c) question:

> Forgiving people is a sign of weakness.

Give **two** reasons why a religious believer might agree or disagree with this statement. (4)

✓ **Check you have learnt:**

- what Christians think about forgiveness
- what Muslims think about forgiveness
- why forgiveness is not a sign of weakness.

**TRY YOUR SKILL AT THIS**

**The (d) question:**

Explain from **two** different religious traditions the teachings about forgiveness.

(You must state the religious tradition you are referring to.) (6)

**Hint**: Use Islam and Christianity and make sure you state clearly which you are talking about each time.

## Case study of a peace activist

In this topic you will examine the work of Archbishop Desmond Tutu.

Here is a detailed look at the work of peace activist Archbishop Desmond Tutu. His efforts to bring peace to South Africa won him the Nobel Peace Prize in 1984, but his work did not stop there. Today, Tutu remains an outspoken campaigner for peace and has travelled to other conflict zones to help peace negotiations. Never one to keep quiet when he knows things are wrong, Tutu recently ruffled a few feathers when he said:

"It would be wonderful if, on behalf of the nation, [President Barack] Obama apologizes to the world, and especially the Iraqis, for an invasion that I believe has turned out to be an unmitigated disaster."

> Some people think reconciliation is a soft option, that it means papering over the cracks. But the biblical meaning means looking facts in the face and it can be very costly; it cost God the death of his own Son.

## Archbishop Tutu

Desmond Tutu was born in South Africa in 1931, at a time when black people were treated as an inferior race by their white rulers. In a system known as 'apartheid' the white government forced two million black people out of their homes so a whites-only zone could be created. Black families had to make homes in broken-down huts with few facilities.

As a young man, Tutu trained as a priest in South Africa and became the first black man to achieve high office in the South African Church. He was outspoken about the suffering of the black people at the hands of their white rulers and, when violence erupted in the black community in Soweto, Tutu had to use his skills to bring peace. The trouble started when the whites tried to stop black people using their own language in black schools. With their language being one of the few things left to them, black people were in uproar. The whites reacted violently to the disturbances and in the ensuing troubles hundreds of black people were killed.

### Activity 1

Why do you think Archbishop Tutu says reconciliation isn't a soft option?

## Non-violent protest

Tutu fully understood the anger of his fellow blacks at the treatment they received but, as a Christian, did not believe violence was the right way forward. He was confident that God would support the poor and oppressed, but insisted Jesus' message was one of love. Tutu urged people to use non-violent protests to draw the world's attention to the suffering of the blacks in South Africa.

Using his position as the first black archbishop of South Africa, Tutu took every opportunity to speak publicly about what was going on, so the world was in no doubt of the injustice. He also led peaceful protests. The rest of the world watched in amazement and horror when Tutu and fellow blacks walked on to a whites-only beach only to be chased off and beaten by police with whips. Tutu also appealed to Britain and other European countries to boycott South African produce in the shops. When sales of apples and grapes slumped, the South African government began losing money and was forced to listen to black people's requests.

By keeping up steady pressure through non-violent means, Tutu and his supporters were able to achieve success in 1994. That was the year South Africa held its first free elections and Nelson Mandela became the first black president. However, the years of bitterness and bloodshed that had taken place to reach this point could not easily be forgotten. White people had abused black people and black people had retaliated with vicious attacks on whites.

*Violent scenes like these where South African police attacked protestors could not easily be forgotten in the new South Africa.*

## Truth and reconciliation

President Mandela asked Tutu to lead the Truth and Reconciliation Committee (TRC), which would look at the terrible things that had happened in the old South Africa. Although people were crying out for revenge, Mandela insisted that there were to be no show trials and executions, but nor could people be expected to 'forgive and forget' the horrors of the past.

People were asked to come forward and tell the truth, either about the crimes they had committed or about what they had suffered. In return for the truth, no matter how terrible it was, that person would be granted an amnesty. Victims would receive the help they needed in return for the truth. Reconciliation meant that everyone had to accept what had happened in the past and not seek revenge.

## A revolutionary way that worked

Tutu, along with others, sat through weeks of harrowing stories and their efforts brought peace and reconciliation to South Africa. Not everyone was able to forget the horrors they suffered and some still wanted revenge, but the bloodbath people predicted never happened.

Tutu has taken his peace-making skills to areas like Northern Ireland, Kenya, the Middle East and Cyprus.

### Activity 2

What was so revolutionary about the way Archbishop Tutu tried to bring about peace?

### Activity 3

Try this (c) question:

Getting people to talk doesn't create peace.

Give **two** reasons why a religious believer might agree or disagree with this statement. (4)

**Check you have learnt:**

- the name of one peace activist
- some of the ways Archbishop Tutu has worked for peace
- the way non-violent methods were used.

**TRY YOUR SKILL AT THIS**

**The (b) question:**

Explain how having a religious faith might encourage a person to work for peace. (4)

In this topic you will examine the way one religious organization is working for peace.

## A united Christian approach to peace in Israel and Palestine

The Ecumenical Accompaniment Programme in Palestine and Israel (EAPPI) was formed in 2002 to work for peace in the troubled region of Israel and Palestine. The problem is that the ownership of this area is disputed. Israel lays claim to the area as the Jewish homeland and the Palestinians lay claim to the area because they have lived there for hundreds of years. The conflict between the two communities causes great suffering to ordinary people on both sides.

EAPPI is made up of Christians from all denominations such as Roman Catholics, Methodists, Baptists, Anglicans and Quakers. What unites them is their opposition to war and the belief that there are better, non-violent ways to resolve conflict and work for world peace.

The organization funds a volunteer accompanier to spend three months living with people on one side of the disputed territory. Because EAPPI supplies accompaniers who live and work with communities on both sides of the disputed territories, they have gained international trust.

The accompanier is an unarmed neutral observer who provides protection by their presence. By just being present, an accompanier can often prevent innocent civilians suffering harassment or human rights abuse. Any breaches of human rights or international and humanitarian law that do occur are reported to the governments of Israel, Palestine and Britain and to the UN. EAPPI volunteers also support the work of peace activists in the communities where they live.

This is how Paul Mukerji, an EAPPI, describes his role:

> We make a difference in small but important ways – helping individuals who had problems with permits, listening to people's stories and frustrations, showing the soldiers that the international community is there to monitor them and report on their actions and behaviour.

### Activity 1

Explain why some Christians think the work of an EAPPI volunteer (who is not armed and has no money to give people) is important in promoting peace.

*Ann Wright is an EAPPI volunteer. Here, she is standing as an observer at one of the checkpoints as two lecturers try to go to work at Nablus University. Although they have the correct ID and permits, two of them are being refused entry.*

## Activity 2

Try this (c) question:

> Religious organizations should keep out of politics.

Give **two** reasons why a religious believer might agree or disagree with this statement. (4)

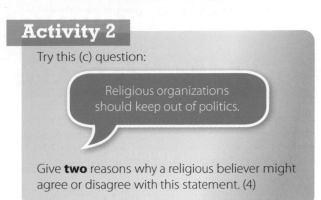

*Liz Burroughs has worked on several EAPPI placements working alongside Muslim and Christian Arab families, as they struggled to maintain their daily life.*

This is what Liz said about the reasons she believes this work is worthwhile:

'As with every war, neither side is totally in the right. It is the ordinary people caught in the middle who suffer. Ecumenical Accompaniers wish to show the ordinary people that the world cares about their suffering. We are Christian ambassadors for peace. We do not take sides, but we are against injustice and human rights abuse. We are not willing to stand by whilst our fellow human beings suffer.

**I listened:** Local people recognized my jacket and knew that I was someone they could talk to about their suffering.

**I watched:** If I saw any abuse of human rights, I reported it.

**I gave support** to those on both sides of the conflict who were working for peace, whatever their race or religion.

**I promised** that when I returned home I would tell their stories as often as I could.'

**Check you have learnt:**

- the name of one religious organization working towards peace
- what this organization does
- why some Christians believe this sort of work matters.

**TRY YOUR SKILL AT THIS**

**The (e) question:**

'Religious organizations aren't likely to create peace.'

Do you agree? Give reasons or evidence for your answer, showing that you have thought of more than one point of view. You must include reference to religious beliefs in your answer. (8 + 5)

## Activity 3

Choose **one** of the following organizations that have worked for peace:

- Corrymeela
- Neve Shalom.

Use the Internet to find out more about it and write an article for a community magazine explaining what the organization does.

# SKILLS COACHING 3

## END OF CHAPTER 1 CHECK

✓ ### Check the (a) question

In the topic *Religion and conflict* we have examined issues of peace, reconciliation, suffering, forgiveness, non-violent protest and attitudes to war. Check you have learnt these **KEY CONCEPTS**:

- conflict
- interfaith dialogue
- just war
- non-violent protest
- pacifism
- reconciliation

✓ ### Check the (b) question

This is where you will be asked how having a religious faith affects someone's response to an issue. Remind yourself of the Christian and the Muslim responses to these issues, but remember that it is also possible to answer from a general religious point of view:

- attitudes towards suffering
- attitudes to conflict and war
- pacifism and non-violent protest
- working towards forgiveness and reconciliation.

✓ ### Check the (d) question

This question is asking you to explain the response of two religious traditions to an issue. You could answer this from a Muslim or Christian viewpoint or you could answer from two traditions within Christianity. Here are a few of the possible areas the (d) question might be concerned with:

- reasons for suffering
- pacifism
- the justification for war
- non-violent protests.

> **Hint:**
> For pacifism you could use two different responses within Christianity if you are clear about how Roman Catholics and members of the Church of England differ on this. Or you could compare a Christian and Muslim response.

✓ ### Check the (c) and (e) questions

The (c) question is where you are offered a controversial statement to comment on. In the (c) question the examiner is asking you to apply what you know about Christian or Muslim attitudes, or a general religious response, to the issues mentioned previously. Don't forget each response needs an example and an explanation.

The (e) question gives you a chance to have your say as well as asking what religious people think about the issue. Obviously, your responses matter. Rehearse two or three reasons you would give to support your viewpoint. These could be examples with an explanation. Remember that you will be assessed on your **Q**uality of **W**ritten **C**ommunication on all (e) questions. For question 1(e), there are 5 extra marks available for spelling, punctuation and the accurate use of grammar.

Revise two or three reasons the other side might give to argue against you.

Finally, the vitally important thing, check that you have referred to religious beliefs. These may relate to one of the religions you have studied; they could relate to another religion you have a good knowledge of, or you might want to make a general point about the way religious believers approach this issue. Whatever you choose, you need to have some examples and explanations ready and state the religion you are referring to.

Here are some stimuli you might be given on an exam paper. Don't ignore them! They are there to help you get thinking.

- Look at each picture and identify what is going on in it. Don't be worried if you notice that it belongs to a religion you haven't studied. The religion is not important, it is what is going on that matters.

- Then look at the questions on the paper and decide which question each picture, or quotation, might apply to.

- Now you can begin to make use of the stimulus. What is the picture telling you about the subject? Does it remind you of any teachings or religious customs you had forgotten, that you might want to use in your answer?

- If the answer is yes, great! Use it in your answer. If the answer is no, that's fine too. It might mean you have already remembered all you need for the answer.

Now try answering these typical examples of Question 1:

(a) Explain what religious believers mean by 'pacifism'. (2)

(b) Explain how having a religious faith might influence someone's attitude about interfaith dialogue. (4)

> Suffering is personal; it has got nothing to do with religion.

(c)

Give two reasons why a religious believer might agree or disagree with this statement. (4)

(i)                                    (ii)

(d) Explain from two different religious traditions the teachings about war.
(You must state the religious traditions you are referring to.) (6)

(i)                                    (ii)

(e) 'Forgiveness is a sign of weakness.'

Do you agree? Give reasons or evidence for your answer, showing that you have thought of more than one point of view. You must include reference to religious beliefs in your answer. (8 + 5)

# CHAPTER 2 Religion and medicine

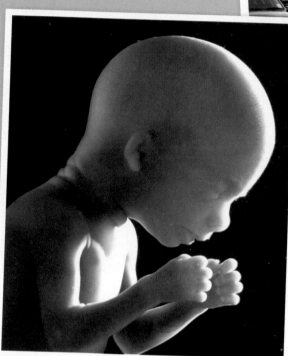

In this topic you will consider some of the reasons why people believe that human life is special.

*As you can see, some people go to great lengths, and great expense, to save one life, even though there are billions of people in the world. This clearly shows that people do think every human life is special.*

## Activity 1

a) What reasons would Paulo, a Christian, give for believing human life is sacred?

b) What reasons would Sarah, an atheist, give for saying human life matters?

## Every life matters

Most people, whether or not they are religious, think that a human life is something special. You have only got to consider the huge efforts doctors and nurses, or people working in the fire and rescue services, put into saving a life.

For religious believers, the reason why human life is special is because it is a gift from God. They use the term **sanctity of life** to refer to their belief that human life is precious. Some believe a human life is of greater value than an animal's because they think God gives humans souls, but not animals.

Most non-believers also think that human life is unique and special. Although they do not believe that God created us, and many do not think there is any life after death, this does not lessen the importance of human life. In fact, some say that human life is so valuable because this is the only life we have. Great efforts should be made to preserve human life and not destroy it.

## Sanctity of life for Christians and Muslims

Both Christianity and Islam believe that human life is God-given. There are many passages in the Bible that tell Christians this is so. St Paul wrote:

 *Don't you know that your body is the temple of the Holy Spirit, who lives in you and who was given to you by God? You do not belong to yourselves but to God.*
**(1 Corinthians 6:19)**

The Qur'an teaches Muslims that Allah deliberately creates a life at the moment of his choosing and breathes life and a soul into that person. At the time of his choosing, God will also take that life back.

 *No one dies unless God wills.* **(Qur'an 3:145)**

Life is sacred for a Muslim because their scriptures teach them that Allah has a plan for the life of every individual from the moment he decides they are conceived.

# The implications of the sanctity of life belief

If someone believes that human life is precious, it will affect how they treat their own body and how they treat other people's bodies. This has huge implications for all stages of human life from conception, through life, to the moment of death and possibly care of that body after death. This chapter is concerned with the impact of the sanctity of life belief. It raises questions such as: does anyone have the right to end another person's life? Does anyone have the right to deny a life by preventing its conception?

> Sanctity of life is a difficult issue in my job. Do you think I should do everything in my power to keep alive the person who has just been brought to hospital by the air ambulance? She has such serious injuries she is likely to remain in a coma and never recover. I'd say she was brain-dead. Should we keep her on life-support?

## Activity 2

Reply to the doctor's question, giving your views about whether the life of the patient who is brain-dead should be preserved at all costs.

## Activity 3

Role-play a conversation between a paramedic from the air ambulance team, who has made great efforts to get to the scene and save the woman's life, and the doctor in the picture.

✓ **Check you have learnt:**

- what is meant by the 'sanctity of life'
- why religious people believe in the sanctity of life
- why non-religious people believe life is precious.

## Activity 4

Try this (c) question:

> Human life must be preserved at all costs.

Give **two** reasons why a religious believer might agree or disagree with this statement. (4)

**TRY YOUR SKILL AT THIS**

**The (e) question:**

'If life belongs to God, nobody should intervene.'

Do you agree? Give reasons or evidence for your answer, showing that you have thought of more than one point of view. You must include reference to religious beliefs in your answer. (8)

## It's my choice

**In this topic you will look at the reasons why some people believe we have a right to personal choice in matters of life and death.**

### KEY CONCEPTS KEY C

**quality of life** the extent to which life is meaningful and pleasurable

**free will** the belief that nothing is determined

**conscience** an innate moral sense that guides actions and responses

I have strong religious beliefs. Okay, I don't go to church and all that, but that doesn't stop me believing that God created me. I would be the first to admit science is stunning and it is possible to grow human tissue in the lab, but we can't create life out of nothing, only God can do that. So that's why we should treat life with great respect. Although we are created by God, we do have **free will**. God didn't make us robots. I think we have the opportunity to decide how we will lead our lives. I have a right to make up my own mind about what happens to my body.

### Activity 2

Explain why some Christians might say free will holds the key to decisions about life and death issues.

I don't have any problems with the idea of the sanctity of life. You would probably call me an agnostic because I'm not sure God exists, but that doesn't make any difference. I still think human life is special – really special. Because of this, it is important to try to lead a happy and fulfilling life. If my life becomes nothing but pain and misery, I don't think I should be forced to carry on. It is the **quality of life** that matters most. I don't want to be kept alive by a machine if everything else has packed up. That can't be right. What matters to me is to have a life that has meaning and pleasure.

### Activity 1

a) What is meant by 'quality of life'?

b) Why do some people think quality of life is a more helpful guide to making life and death decisions than sanctity of life?

When I have got a difficult personal decision to make, I find it helps to talk to friends and family. You get the benefit of other people's experience. Religion can be helpful, I suppose. I could ask the local vicar because he has got training and knowledge of the scriptures, but I think people who know me well are going to be the most helpful.

When it comes to making up your mind about the right course of action, I think you should follow your **conscience**. We have all got a conscience that tells us right from wrong. I know it is reliable, though I admit I don't always do what it tells me! Frankly, I would rather trust my own conscience when it comes to serious issues than be dictated to by any religion. Their holy books may have got it wrong, perhaps have been translated incorrectly or are just out of date. For me, conscience is the best guide to the correct course of action. Some people say that God is the one who is informing my conscience. Well, maybe. I don't know, but I am sure that my conscience gives me the best moral guidance.

## Activity 4

Try this (c) question:

If everybody obeyed their conscience, we wouldn't need any rules.

Give **two** reasons why a religious believer might agree or disagree with this statement. (4)

### ✓ Check you have learnt:

- what is meant by 'quality of life'
- why conscience may be a useful guide to making moral decisions
- what is meant by 'free will'.

### TRY YOUR SKILL AT THIS

**The (b) question:**
Explain how having a religious faith might influence someone's choices in matters of life and death. (4)

## Activity 3

Why does Zara think it is best to listen to her conscience when it comes to difficult moral decisions? Do you think it would have helped the doctor on page 41 with her decision to treat the accident victim? Why?

# 2.3 Doctors' dilemma

## KEY CONCEPTS

**medical ethics** the moral principles that affect medical issues and practice

**Hippocratic Oath** a special promise made by those working in medicine to do their best to preserve life

*These medical students are graduating after many years of study. What four things do you think they should be asked to promise in their new jobs as doctors?*

## The problems of a modern doctor

Doctors are the people we go to for advice when our body isn't working as well as we would like. We expect doctors to be honest, helpful and sympathetic. Actually, being honest and sympathetic may be the easiest part of their job. Giving the right help may be more difficult, as the story of the road accident victim on page 40 shows. Knowing what drugs and medical techniques are available is one thing, but deciding whether it is right to use such treatment to prolong a life is another matter.

What if the doctor and patient disagree about a certain treatment? Who should finally decide? The doctor has years of experience and medical training, but the patient surely has rights over their own body. **Medical ethics** is the term given to the difficult decisions doctors are sometimes faced with about whether it is right or wrong to carry out a certain procedure. Two examples of difficult decisions are featured on these pages.

A newly qualified doctor makes a special promise, known as the **Hippocratic Oath**, to use their skills to do their best to preserve a person's life. Today, this oath takes the form of a set of standards laid out by the General Medical Council (GMC).

This is how a modern UK doctor is expected to behave according to the GMC:

- Make the care of your patient your first concern.
- Protect and promote the health of patients and the public.
- Provide a good standard of practice and care:
  - keep your professional knowledge and skills up to date
  - recognize and work within the limits of your competence
  - work with colleagues in the ways that best serve patients' interests.
- Treat patients as individuals and respect their dignity:
  - treat patients politely and considerately
  - respect patients' right to confidentiality.
- Work in partnership with patients:
  - listen to patients and respond to their concerns and preferences
  - give patients the information they want or need in a way they can understand
  - respect patients' right to reach decisions with you about their treatment and care
  - support patients in caring for themselves to improve and maintain their health.
- Be honest and open and act with integrity:
  - act without delay if you have good reason to believe that you or a colleague may be putting patients at risk
  - never discriminate unfairly against patients or colleagues
  - never abuse your patients' trust in you or the public's trust in the profession.

## Activity 1

Read the points set out by the GMC about a doctor's behaviour. Which points might guide the doctor treating the road accident patient on page 40?

# TWINS' MUM DIES FOR HER BELIEFS

Twenty-two-year-old Emma Gough died just hours after giving birth to twins at the Royal Shrewsbury Hospital. As a Jehovah's Witness, she had signed a form refusing a blood transfusion before the birth and the hospital was powerless to intervene.

After a normal delivery, Emma suffered a massive loss of blood. Medics begged her husband and family to overrule her decision and let her have blood, but they refused.

*6 November 2007*

## Activity 2

a) Explain why doctors treating Emma Gough faced a difficult decision. If you were Emma's doctor, what would you have done and why?

b) A Dublin court recently overruled the mother in a similar case to Emma Gough's and told the doctors to give the mother blood because her child has a right to a mother. Was that the right decision?

# LET'S FACE IT

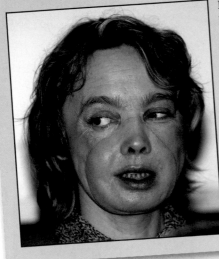

Isabelle Dinoire had a successful partial face transplant in 2005. When her nose, lips and chin were torn off by a dog, French surgeons realized the injuries were too severe to repair. Instead, they made medical history with the world's first facial transplant.

## Activity 3

Try this (c) question:

> If the doctors can do it, then it must be right.

Give **two** reasons why a religious believer might agree or disagree with this statement. (4)

**Check you have learnt:**

- what the Hippocratic Oath is
- what is meant by 'medical ethics'
- two examples of ethical dilemmas doctors might face.

**TRY YOUR SKILL AT THIS**

**The (e) question:**

'Doctors should do what the patient asks them to do.'

Do you agree? Give reasons or evidence for your answer, showing that you have thought of more than one point of view. You must include reference to religious beliefs in your answer. (8)

Transplant surgery is one area where medical science has made huge advances. It is now routine for doctors to transplant a cornea, a lung or a heart successfully, but is it right to transplant a face? Do you think doctors should be allowed to transplant animal organs into a human, or to perform a brain transplant?

## DO YOU UNDERSTAND?

### Improve your skill with the (a) question

In this topic so far you have learnt six **KEY CONCEPTS**:

- conscience (page 43)
- Hippocratic Oath (page 44)
- quality of life (page 42)
- free will (page 42)
- sanctity of life (page 40)
- medical ethics (page 44)

One way to gain 2 marks every time is to learn the exact definition that is given. Can you recite it word for word? Don't worry if you can't manage it, other wording is acceptable so long as it means exactly the same thing. Can you write down the definition of each key concept without looking back?

### Improve your skill with the (b) question

This question is asking you to **make links** between what a religion teaches and how a person behaves.

Remember this useful way of tackling the (b) question:

**POINT + EXAMPLE + EXPLANATION**

This is also a question that rewards the use of **specialist language**; in fact you have to use it to get more than 1 mark.

Let's analyse this (b) question:

> Explain how having a religious faith might support the view that life is special.

There are two parts to the (b) answer:

- What does the religion, or religions, teach about the value of life?
- What is the evidence? In other words, how do believers behave?

You need to link these parts together in order to gain full marks.

CHECK OUT THE TERMS

Check your answer to make sure you have included either specialist language or key concepts. Unusually, all the key concepts have come at the start of this chapter. You have learnt terms like 'sanctity of life', 'quality of life', 'free will', 'conscience', 'Hippocratic Oath' and 'medical ethics'. Choose the most appropriate ones to work into your answer so you can access the highest level on the mark scheme.

USING THE STIMULUS

When you open the first page of every topic on the exam paper, you will see an array of coloured pictures and sometimes a quotation or a diagram. These are there to give you some assistance, to stimulate your memory. For the topic **Religion and medicine** that we are currently studying, you might see pictures of a person with a test tube or someone in a wheelchair. There could be pictures of members of a religious group protesting with banners.

If there is a statement on the stimulus page, read it. It might nudge you to include something in an answer. It is also possible that you may decide it's not relevant to what you want to say. No problem, ignore it in that case.

### STEP 1

Choose the religion, or religions, you want to write about.

Now write the **basic point** that religion teaches.

*The … religion teaches that people are made by God.* = 1 mark

### STEP 2

Now **add an example**.

*The … religion teaches that men and women are made by God so human life is special.* = 2 marks

### STEP 3

Now **add an explanation**.

*The … religion teaches that men and women are made by God so human life is special because it is God given.* = 3 marks

### STEP 4

To get up to Level 4 and receive 4 marks you need to give a second example which would be worth 2 marks in its own right.

# WHAT DO PEOPLE THINK?

## Improve your skill with the (c) question

You are probably becoming quite familiar with these controversial little statements that turn up in a speech bubble on each double page. They are there to get you thinking and arguing. A good preparation for answering the (c) question (and incidentally the (e) question because a similar statement could turn up as an (e) question too) is to have a class debate about the statement or you could simply discuss it with a neighbour. Make notes of the different views people put forward on this topic and keep them safe as revision aids. You never know!

When a statement turns up in a speech bubble on the exam paper you know that the examiner wants you to explain what religious believers think about an issue. Under the speech bubble it will say:

**Give two reasons why a religious believer might agree or disagree with this statement. (4)**

Here is a typical (c) question:

> Doctors must do what the patient wants.

**Give two reasons why a religious believer might agree or disagree with this statement. (4)**

Let's tackle the (c) question step by step:

### STEP 4

Choose two religious examples to use in your answer. Choose the ones that you can explain the most fully.

FINALLY, write up your answer. You could begin: *'The ... religion would agree/disagree with this statement for two reasons ...'* then give your example and explanation for each one as fully as you can.

### STEP 3

What are the religious teachings on this subject? Note them down. Does it look like the religion will be totally in agreement or disagreement? Or might there be different interpretations on this issue?

### STEP 2

Choose which religion, or religions, or general religious viewpoints you are going to use in your answer. Write them down.

### STEP 1

Underline the important words in the statement. <u>Doctors must do</u> what the <u>patient wants</u>.

**In this topic you will consider the different rights of people involved in decisions about abortion.**

### Useful specialist language

**pro-life** those who do not agree with abortion because they believe the foetus has the right to life

**pro-choice** those who believe the mother has the right to choose whether or not she has an abortion

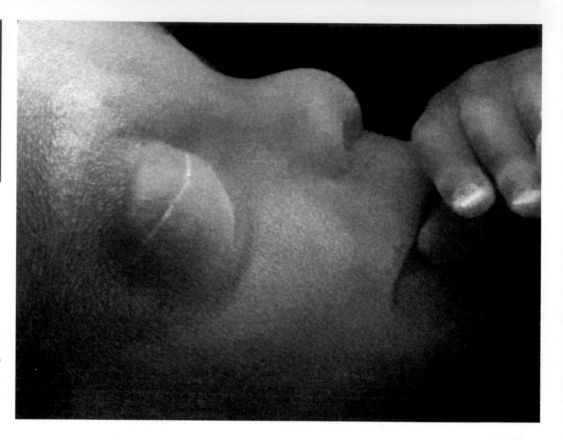

*This is a 12-week-old foetus. Do you see a baby or a cluster of developing cells? Discuss why this distinction could matter when it comes to decisions about abortion.*

## What is abortion?

Abortion means deliberately removing a foetus from the womb before it can survive. This is a deliberate action in order to end the life of the foetus. Not surprisingly, it is a very controversial issue. In May 2008 Parliament debated whether the abortion time limit of 24 weeks should be reduced.

### Activity 1

Go to the BBC News website for 21 May 2008. Find out exactly what MPs were asked to vote on. Write down the points each side offered in support of their argument. Who won? Which side would you have voted for? Why?

### Activity 2

For debate: Is the plan for 'lunch-hour abortions' a good thing or a bad thing?

## LUNCH-HOUR ABORTIONS CAUSE OUTRAGE

Plans to permit women to be able to walk into a clinic, have a ten-minute abortion in their lunch break for £300, then go back to work, provoked a furious reaction. One person said, "[Y]ou have fast food and now you can have a fast abortion. It horrifies me".

A spokeswoman for the clinic said they aimed to 'remove the stigma' from abortion for women who were less than 12 weeks pregnant. Their service was designed to fit into a woman's busy working life.

*June 1997*

# Pro-life

Some people believe abortion is wrong because a foetus is a life that already possesses the full DNA to develop into a unique person. People against abortion are often called **pro-life** because they put the life and rights of the unborn child first.

# Pro-choice

Others argue that it is a woman's right to choose what happens to her body. This view can be called **pro-choice**. A woman might seek an abortion because her health will suffer, or because her unborn child is likely to be so handicapped it will have a poor quality of life. Or she may not be in a position to look after a child properly.

# What is legal in Britain?

A woman does not have an automatic right to an abortion in Britain. Two doctors must agree that:

- the mother is less than 24 weeks pregnant
- the mother's physical or mental health is at risk
- the baby is likely to be born severely physically or mentally handicapped
- the birth would have a seriously bad effect on other children in the family.

# The sanctity of life or the quality of life?

Those against abortion say that it is wrong to kill unborn babies. They ask what right we have to dispose of a life because it's inconvenient, or not up to the standard we expected. Human life is special and killing it is murder.

Others argue that it is the quality of life that matters. If either the mother or the baby is going to suffer a miserable or painful life if the pregnancy continues, then abortion should be allowed.

## Activity 3

Try this (c) question:

> It's my body; I don't need anyone's permission to do what I like with it.

Give **two** reasons why a religious believer might agree or disagree with this statement. (4)

## Activity 4

Read this list of possible people involved in decisions about an abortion:

- the father
- the potential grandparents
- the doctor who will carry out the abortion
- members of a religion
- the mother.

Write down why each would claim they have a right to have their views heard. Then rank them in order of priority. Does the foetus have any rights to be considered? Gianna certainly thought so.

*Gianna Jessen survived an abortion in the final three months of her 17-year-old mother's pregnancy. Gianna was born weighing 2lbs and with cerebral palsy, but now runs marathons to raise money for sufferers. She said, "If abortion is about women's rights, then what were my rights?"*

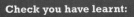

## Check you have learnt:

- what legal right a woman has to an abortion in the UK
- how the sanctity of life and the quality of life arguments can be applied to abortion
- why some people think the unborn child does have rights.

## TRY YOUR SKILL AT THIS

**The (e) question:**

'A woman should not be able to ask for an abortion.'

Do you agree? Give reasons or evidence for your answer, showing that you have thought of more than one point of view. You must include reference to religious beliefs in your answer. (8)

## What do Christians think about abortion?

In 2005 an Anglican priest, the Reverend Joanna Jepson, took the police to court for failing to prosecute two doctors who permitted a late abortion on the grounds that the foetus had a cleft palate. Joanna herself had been born with a cleft palate and more serious facial defects but had undergone surgery to have them corrected. She argued the abortion was illegal because a cleft palate is not a serious enough handicap to permit a late abortion. (Look back to page 49 to check the legal position.) Joanna said, "For me, an abortion of any foetus – let alone one that is seven months old – for what is a treatable facial condition, can never be morally justified."

*Reverend Joanna Jepson was born with a serious facial deformity that has been corrected by surgery.*

### Did being a Christian mean Joanna could never permit an abortion?

**Activity 1**

Would you have allowed that seven-month abortion? Give **two** reasons for your answer.

The answer is actually no. Although Christians believe firmly in the sanctity of life and are against killing one of God's creations, some liberal Protestants believe there are occasions when it might be kinder to allow an abortion than insist the pregnancy continues.

Their argument is that Jesus taught his followers that love is the most important thing and any situation should be judged on that. If a baby is likely to be born with crippling deformities that mean it would have a short painful life, it might be more loving to abort the foetus at an early stage to prevent suffering. In another case, some might say it is kinder to allow a woman to have an abortion than suffer a complicated birth that could threaten her life or make her very ill. Some Christians believe it is impossible to give one judgement for all situations; they say judgements should be based on what is the most loving thing to do in the circumstances.

> *Dear friends let us love one another, because love comes from God. Whoever loves is a child of God and knows God. Whoever does not love does not know God, for God is love.* **(1 John 4:7–8)**

### The Roman Catholic teaching

> *From the first moment of his existence, a human being must be recognized as having the rights of a person – among which is the inviolable right of every innocent being to life.*
> **(Catechism of the Catholic Church 2270)**

**Activity 2**

Examine each Bible passage in turn. Explain why each would teach a Christian not to accept abortion.

Roman Catholics believe that a person's life begins immediately after an egg is fertilized by a sperm. From that moment, a person has the right to life, which no one can take away from them for any reason. Roman Catholics support their view with biblical teachings like these:

**a**  *Do not commit murder.* **(Exodus 20:13)**

**b** *Children are a gift from the lord; they are a real blessing.* **(Psalm 127:3)**

**c** *God created human beings making them to be like himself.* **(Genesis 1:27)**

# The Anglican teaching

This is what the Church of England said about the grounds for permitting abortion.

'In situations where the continuance of a pregnancy threatens the life of the mother a termination of pregnancy may be justified.'

They urge support for the medical profession: 'In efforts to ensure that, when abortion has to be undertaken, it is carried out as early in the pregnancy as possible.'

They also went on to say:

'That in the rare occasions when abortion is carried out beyond 24 weeks, "serious foetal handicap" should be interpreted strictly as applying to those conditions where survival is possible only for a very short period.'

## Activity 3

Try this (c) question:

> Christians should never allow abortion.

Give **two** reasons why a religious believer might agree or disagree with this statement. (4)

## Activity 4

Read the placards these protestors are carrying. Which might be carried by supporters of the sanctity of life and which by those supporting the quality of life argument? Explain what religious reason they would give for their views.

**Check you have learnt:**

- why some Christians might support abortion
- why some Christians would never support abortion
- why some Christians say it depends on the circumstances.

**TRY YOUR SKILL AT THIS**

**The (b) question:**

Explain how having a religious faith might influence a person's attitude towards abortion. (4)

**In this topic you will look at different Muslim attitudes towards abortion and the reasons for them.**

*Abortion creates strong opinions amongst Muslims, but Islam does not totally forbid it.*

## Only Allah gives and takes life

The Qur'an teaches Muslims that life is a gift from Allah and should be treated with great respect. You will recognize this belief as the sanctity of life (see page 40). No Muslim likes the idea of abortion because it involves taking a life given by Allah and that is wrong. There are, however, different approaches to abortion in Islam that hinge on the decision about exactly when a foetus becomes a person.

### Activity 1

 *No one dies unless God wills. The term of every life is fixed.*
**(Qur'an 3:145)**

What do you think this quotation from the Qur'an teaches Muslims about abortion?

For some Muslims, this quotation means that all human life is a gift from Allah and a foetus is life from the moment of conception. This means we do not own any life; it is on loan to us from Allah and is not ours to destroy. This means abortion is totally unacceptable to these Muslims.

### Activity 2

Try this (c) question:

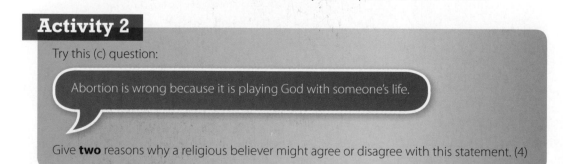

Abortion is wrong because it is playing God with someone's life.

Give **two** reasons why a religious believer might agree or disagree with this statement. (4)

# Ensoulment

Most Muslims believe that Allah puts a soul into the foetus when it is 120 days old (17 weeks). This is the defining moment when a cluster of developing cells becomes a human. Until **ensoulment**, a mother has greater rights than her unborn child. Although no Muslim likes to destroy a life, some will permit abortion before ensoulment if there is a compelling reason. It might be that the mother's health is suffering. Some liberal Muslims might also permit abortion before ensoulment if the child is likely to be born physically or mentally disabled.

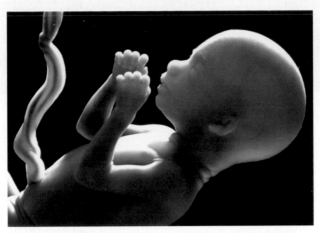

*This foetus is 120 days old, the age when Muslims believe Allah breathes a soul into it.*

Islam does not allow an abortion because the baby would be inconvenient, or the family does not think it can afford another child. In fact, the Qur'an makes it clear that Muslims should trust in Allah to provide for the child.

> *You shall not kill your children for fear of want. We will provide for them and for you. To kill them is a grievous sin.* **(Qur'an 17:31)**

# The rights of the mother

After 120 days, abortion is rarely permitted unless there is a risk to the woman's life if her pregnancy continues. In a situation like this abortion would be permitted because it is seen as the lesser of two evils. Because the mother is already alive and probably has responsibilities for a family, her death would cause greater suffering to the family than the death of an unborn child. It is also probable that if she died, the foetus would die anyway.

Abortion is never undertaken lightly. The Qur'an warns Muslim mothers who have an abortion that in the afterlife they will come face to face with their unborn child. That child will ask them why they were killed.

**Check you have learnt:**

- how ensoulment might affect decisions about abortion
- two reasons why Muslims might permit abortion
- two reasons why Muslims might disagree with abortion.

## Activity 3

Draw two columns on your page, one headed 'For' and the other 'Against'. In the 'For' column, write the reasons why some Muslims might permit an abortion. In the 'Against' column, write the reasons why some Muslims are against abortion.

## Activity 4

Read this letter in a magazine.

Reply to Aisha telling her what the Islamic teachings on this are. You can tell her your own views so long as you back them up with reasons.

> I am a happily married Muslim woman but I am really worried about having another baby. I am ten weeks pregnant and we already have three children. I don't think we can afford a fourth one. Is it wrong for me to have an abortion?
>
> *Aisha*

**TRY YOUR SKILL AT THIS**

**The (e) question:**

'Religious people shouldn't agree to an abortion.'

Do you agree? Give reasons or evidence for your answer, showing that you have thought of more than one point of view. You must include reference to religious beliefs in your answer. (8)

**Hint**: Use the table from Activity 3 to help you answer this question.

# 2.7

**Whose life is it anyway?**

In this topic you will consider the dilemmas raised by euthanasia.

## Activity 1

a) The court rejected Diane Pretty's request but granted Miss B's. Why are the two cases different? Do you think the decisions were correct?

b) Write down the judgement you would give on each case and **two** reasons why.

### CASE 1

In 2002, Diane Pretty was suffering from motor neuron disease and faced the possibility of a painful death. She asked the court's permission for her husband to assist her to commit suicide (**assisted suicide**) without him risking prosecution and 14 years in prison. What Mrs Pretty asked for was to be allowed to die with dignity at a time of her choosing.

### CASE 2

At the same time, Miss B's lawyers went to court to ask permission for her to have her life-support machine switched off. Although her mental functions were undamaged, she was paralysed from the neck downwards and had no hope of recovery. Miss B argued that her quality of life was so poor, being kept alive by a machine was worse than being dead.

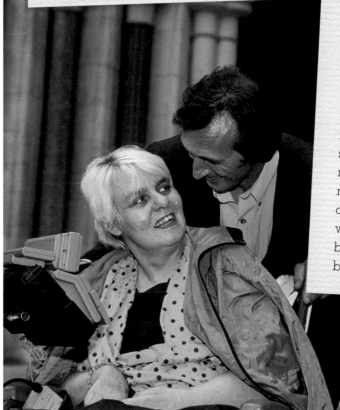

*Diane Pretty and her husband Brian outside the High Court. She asked for the right for her husband to help her commit suicide legally.*

### Useful specialist language

**assisted suicide** providing a seriously ill person with the means to commit suicide

**euthanasia** the painless killing of someone dying from a painful disease

**voluntary euthanasia** ending life painlessly when someone in great pain asks for death

**non-voluntary euthanasia** ending someone's life painlessly when they are unable to ask, but you have good reason for thinking they would want you to do so

## What is euthanasia?

Both case studies involve **euthanasia**, which some people describe as 'mercy killing' because it involves deliberately ending another person's life to prevent them from suffering.

● **Voluntary euthanasia** is when a patient asks someone to end their life so they can escape pain and suffering. It might involve asking the doctor for a lethal overdose or asking relatives to deliberately leave a large supply of drugs within their reach. Voluntary euthanasia is illegal in Britain and in most of Europe.

● **Non-voluntary euthanasia** occurs when someone ends a patient's life without their permission, to avoid further suffering. This might occur if the patient was in a coma and being kept alive by a life-support machine even though they were 'brain-dead'. Decisions like this may require the permission of a court.

# Why would anyone want euthanasia?

Some people request euthanasia because their quality of life is already poor and will only get worse because of a terminal illness. Unbearable pain or the loss of personal dignity might be involved because everything from feeding to going to the toilet requires assistance. The patient might want to die peacefully with their family around them, rather than carry on suffering as their loved ones watch helplessly.

**Those in favour of euthanasia say:**

It is your life, so why shouldn't you be allowed to make decisions about it?

If an animal was suffering, euthanasia would be the obvious kindness. Why can't a human be shown the same consideration?

It is a waste of money keeping a hopeless case alive in hospital when the money could be better spent on those with a chance of recovery.

However, taking someone's life, whether they ask for it or not, is a very controversial thing.

**Those against euthanasia say:**

Nearly everyone believes in the sanctity of human life even if they are not religious.

Doctors are human and they can make mistakes when diagnosing an illness, but, even if they're right, cures are being discovered all the time. Modern drugs are powerful enough to control pain. And think about doctors. It is wrong to ask them to kill a person when their training is for saving life.

If euthanasia was legal, elderly relatives might feel pressured into asking to be 'put to sleep' because they are a nuisance to the family.

## Activity 2

Try this (c) question:

Free will means I can choose when to end my life.

Give **two** reasons why a religious believer might agree or disagree with this statement. (4)

## Activity 3

List at least **four** people who might feel their views should be heard in the case of an elderly aunt requesting euthanasia. Who would you take the most notice of and why?

### CASE 3

The case of *Superman* actor Christopher Reeve shows how controversial euthanasia is. He suffered terrible injuries after a riding accident in 1995 that left him in a coma and on life support. Doctors said that if he survived, he would be paralysed from the neck down and unable to breathe on his own. His mother wanted the machine switched off. His wife and the doctors wanted to wait and see if he would wake up and maybe express his wishes. He did come round and, although he initially wanted the machine switched off, changed his mind. He later had a pioneering operation to reconnect his spinal column and, although he remained in a wheelchair, recovered feeling in 70% of his body. He died in 2004.

### Check you have learnt:

- the difference between two types of euthanasia
- two reasons why people are in favour of euthanasia
- two reasons why people are against euthanasia.

### TRY YOUR SKILL AT THIS

**The (e) question:**

'Euthanasia is just another name for murder.'

Do you agree? Give reasons or evidence for your answer, showing that you have thought of more than one point of view. You must include reference to religious beliefs in your answer. (8)

### Improve your skill with the (b) question

Using the skills that you have learnt already, choose one of the questions below to answer. Aim to get 4 marks by either developing your explanation as fully as possible or by using two examples. Don't forget to use some specialist language.

Remember: **POINT + EXAMPLE + EXPLANATION**

If you do this twice, it will lead you up to the highest level.

Explain how a religious faith might influence a person's attitude towards preserving a life. (4)

Explain how having a religious faith might encourage some believers to accept abortion. (4)

### Improve your skill with the (d) question

This is one of the big questions on the paper because it is worth 6 marks. This question is asking you to take one issue and write about the way two religions, or two traditions within the same religion, react to this issue. Concentrate on analysing the responses because that holds the key to improving your mark.

A typical question might start: *Explain from two different religious traditions ... .*

A question relating to the work in this chapter might ask you to:

Explain from two different religious traditions the teachings about abortion. (6)

Let's tackle this (d) question step by step:

**STEP 1** Look at the question and underline what it is asking about: in this case abortion. Look at the stimulus on the paper (or in this case on pages 50–53) to see if there is anything there that might help you.

**STEP 2** Write down the **two** different religious traditions you are going to use. Will it be Christianity and Islam or do you want to consider two different views within Christianity? For example, there are Christians who believe abortion is never acceptable and others who believe that sometimes it may be the kinder option.

**STEP 3** Start with the first religion. Write down one basic teaching about abortion. = 1 mark

**STEP 4** Now develop that teaching with an example. That should add 1 mark more. = 2 marks

**STEP 5** Can you develop that point further, either by discussing it in detail or by adding another example?

Is there any specialist language you can include to show the examiner you have a good grasp of the subject?

**STEP 6** Repeat the procedure for your second religious tradition.

*Tip:*
It is best to aim to give two examples in your development for both religions you are discussing, if you want to get the full marks on offer.

To see how the examiner will mark your answer, look at the mark scheme on page 24.

# WHAT DO PEOPLE THINK?

## Improve your skill with the (e) question

In the (c) question you were given a speech bubble containing a controversial statement that asked for a religious response. The (e) question is building on this because it is asking for a religious response and your views on this subject. At last, the opportunity for you to have your say and give your reasons!

This question is also testing whether you can understand someone else's point of view that differs from your own. Because a lot is being asked in (e) questions there are 8 marks given for your answer. This is the largest number of marks for any part of a question, so it is well worth improving your skills here.

Here is a typical (e) question.

'Decisions about birth and death should be left to God.'

Do you agree? Give reasons or evidence for your answer, showing that you have thought of more than one point of view. You must include reference to religious beliefs in your answer. (8)

Let's tackle the (e) question step by step:

### STEP 1

Draw two columns on your page and head one side 'Agree' and the other side 'Disagree'. Write two or three points in each column. Check that some of them are religious views. You might like to write the name of the religion, or the religious denomination, against it. If you feel that most religious believers think this, then you can note that down. You don't have to specify which religion if you don't feel it is appropriate; just say 'Most religious believers ...' if you know this is true and have the evidence to support it.

### STEP 2

Look at the columns you have drawn up and note alongside what examples you could give for each of those points. Put an asterisk against the examples you could explain in detail. Clearly they are the best ones to choose in your answer!

Check what specialist language you can include. Are there any key concepts you could use?

### STEP 3

Use the method of:

**POINT + EXAMPLE + EXPLANATION.**

You learnt, on page 46, to write two paragraphs, one for each viewpoint.

It is often easier to begin with your own view. The more you develop this view the better.

Then repeat the format for the second paragraph that is going to explain why some people do not agree with this view.

In this topic you will look at different Christian attitudes to euthanasia and the reasons for them.

## Christian belief

Christians believe that God created human life and made it superior to other animal life. They believe that life is a gift from God and, for that reason, all human life is sacred. Added to that, in the Genesis account of creation it states that God made humans in his image. For Christians, this means nobody has the right to take either their own life or that of another person, even if asked to do so. Biblical teachings lead most Christians to reject euthanasia as wrong.

### Activity 1

a) Copy down the biblical passages below and underline the important sections for a Christian looking for guidance on euthanasia.

b) Explain what the Bible teaches Christians about euthanasia.

> *The Lord kills and restores to life; he sends people to the world of the dead and brings them back again.*
> **(1 Samuel 2:6)**

> *None of us lives for himself only, none of us dies for himself only. If we live, it is for the Lord that we live, and if we die, it is for the Lord that we die.* **(Romans 14:7–8)**

> *Don't you know that your body is the temple of the Holy Spirit, who lives in you and who was given to you by God? You do not belong to yourselves but to God.*
> **(1 Corinthians 6:19)**

> *Do not commit murder.* **(Exodus 20:13)**

*If you think humans are related to apes, would you permit humans to be put to sleep when they are old in the same way as an animal? Why?*

## Different Christian approaches to euthanasia

Whilst Christians agree that life is God-given and taking it is wrong, there are some differences of opinion about precisely when life ends.

For some, it is acceptable to switch off a life-support machine if there is medical evidence that the patient is 'brain-dead'. This is because they believe the person has already died and the machine is only performing mechanical bodily functions.

Some Christians are also prepared to consider withholding treatment that might prolong life when a person's quality of life is already very poor. They are guided by Jesus' teaching that what really matters is to act in the most loving way towards another person. That could involve respecting their decision to refuse treatment or to end their life.

The views above would only be considered by liberal Christians; the Roman Catholic Church is totally against euthanasia in any form. They do, however, accept that a person has the right to refuse treatment that merely prolongs life and accept that life is coming to a natural end.

## The Hospice offers Christians a real alternative to euthanasia

The Hospice movement began in England when a Christian doctor, Cicely Saunders, refused to accept the idea of euthanasia and set about finding an alternative. Having specialized in pain relief, Cicely believed that if a patient's pain could be controlled, it was possible for them to enjoy a good quality of life, even when suffering from a terminal illness.

Hospice care is concerned not just with nursing, but also with making a person's final weeks or days comfortable, calm and happy. Cicely Saunders said: "You matter because you are you, and you matter to the last moment of your life." The hospice also supports the whole family with emotional, spiritual and practical help.

Since the opening of the first hospice in London in 1967, the movement has spread with over 220 hospices in the UK and 8000 worldwide. In recognition of her work, Cicely Saunders was made a Dame in 1980. She died in 2005. As a Christian, Dame Cicely believed that birth and death are a natural part of life and she said we should 'concern ourselves with the quality of life as well as its length'. What did she mean by that?

### Activity 2

Read these two statements:

(i) 'Whatever its motives and means, direct euthanasia consists in putting an end to the lives of handicapped, sick, or dying persons. It is morally unacceptable. Thus an act or omission which, of itself or by intention, causes death in order to eliminate suffering constitutes a murder gravely contrary to the dignity of the human person and to the respect due to the living God, his Creator.' (Catechism of the Catholic Church 2277).

(ii) 'The Roman Catholic Church does not, however, argue that life must be preserved at all cost. 'Discontinuing medical procedures that are burdensome, dangerous, extraordinary, or disproportionate to the expected outcome can be legitimate; it is the refusal of "over-zealous" treatment. Here one does not will to cause death; one's inability to impede it is merely accepted.' (Catechism of the Catholic Church 2278)

a) What does statement (i) tell Catholics about voluntary euthanasia and what reason is given?

b) Statement (ii) relates to non-voluntary euthanasia. What guidance is given here?

### Activity 3

Try this (c) question:

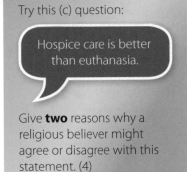

> Hospice care is better than euthanasia.

Give **two** reasons why a religious believer might agree or disagree with this statement. (4)

### Activity 4

Draw a diagram to show the different attitudes Christians have to euthanasia with a brief reason for each.

✓ **Check you have learnt:**

- two reasons why some Christians reject euthanasia
- two reasons why some Christians might consider euthanasia
- why the hospice offers an alternative to euthanasia.

**TRY YOUR SKILL AT THIS**

**The (e) question:**

'Allowing euthanasia is the kindest thing to do.'

Do you agree? Give reasons or evidence for your answer, showing that you have thought of more than one point of view. You must include reference to religious beliefs in your answer. (8)

In this topic you will look at Muslim attitudes to euthanasia and the reasons for them.

Muslims believe life is a gift from Allah. This makes it sacred and to be cherished and protected at all times. The Qur'an says:

> It is He who has given you life, and He who will cause you to die and make you live again. Surely man is ungrateful. **(Qur'an 22:66)**

The European Council for Fatwa & Research, which advises Muslims, has stated: 'It is forbidden to end deliberately (by intention) or to hasten the death of any person.'

The Qur'an says:

> Do not kill yourselves. God is merciful to you. **(Qur'an 4:29)**

Allah has a plan for everyone. Only he decides the length of a person's life and the time they will die.

> No one dies unless God wills. The term of every life is fixed. **(Qur'an 3:145)**

> When their time arrives, not for one hour shall they stay behind: nor can they go before it. **(Qur'an 16:61)**

Muslims regard euthanasia as a form of suicide and Muhammad taught that all forms of suicide are wrong. Anyone involved in suicide will be punished in the afterlife.

Muhammad told Muslims about a soldier who was wounded in battle and committed suicide.

> Amongst the nations before you there was a man who got a wound, and growing impatient (with its pain) he took a knife and cut his wrist with it and the blood did not stop till he died. Allah said, 'My slave hurried to bring death upon himself so I have forbidden him to enter Paradise.' **(Hadith)**

**Muslims believe euthanasia is wrong**

Muslims believe that life is set as a test by Allah and everyone will be judged on the way they lived their life. Asking for euthanasia is trying to cheat by speeding up the test.

> Believers, fortify yourselves with patience and prayer. God is with those that are patient. **(Qur'an 2:153)**

## Activity 1

Use the information on this page and on pages 40–41 (sanctity of life) to make a list of the reasons why Muslims are against euthanasia.

**Activity 2**

This child is on a life-support machine but there is no likelihood he will recover. How would you respond to the family's request to switch the machine off?

Give your reasons.

Would a Muslim agree with your decision? Why?

## Sanctity of life

Muslims believe that euthanasia is wrong because it contradicts Allah's teachings about the sanctity of life. They also believe that, no matter what state the body is in, the soul is perfect and that is what matters to Allah. Because life is a test and Allah is never unfair, we cannot know the reason why a person suffers. What Muslims are sure of is that anyone who is suffering should be treated with love and compassion until the end of their natural life. Islam teaches that we will be judged in the afterlife on the care we showed to those in need.

## A recent ruling on euthanasia

Muslim lawyers have responded to advances in medical technology that can keep a person's body alive when it would have died naturally. They have agreed that it is permissible for patients in a coma who are kept alive by life-support machines, but without any hope of recovery, to have the machine switched off. This is because their life has already ended and the machine is of no use.

Palliative care (a form of nursing that involves controlling a person's pain when healing is impossible) is recommended in Islam. The best hospice care for a Muslim, it is said, is at home surrounded by family.

**Check you have learnt:**

- two reasons why some Christians reject euthanasia
- why Muslims might be permitted to switch off a life-support machine
- how the sanctity of life argument might be applied.

**Activity 3**

Try this (c) question:

> Euthanasia is always wrong.

Give **two** reasons why a religious believer might agree or disagree with this statement. (4)

**TRY YOUR SKILL AT THIS**

**The (d) question:**

Explain from **two** different religious traditions the teachings about euthanasia. (You must state the religious traditions you are referring to.) (6)

**In this topic you will look at some people's responses to the issue of in vitro fertilization.**

**Useful specialist language**

**in vitro fertilization (IVF)** the method of fertilizing a human egg in a laboratory

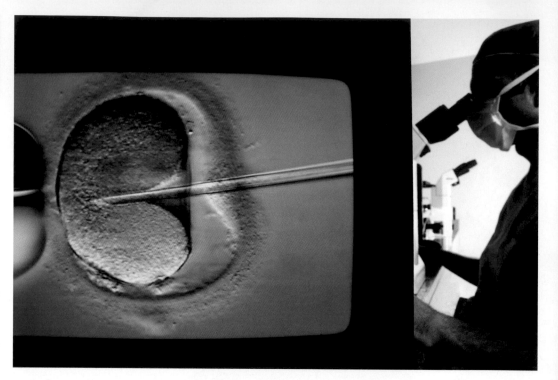

*An egg that has been taken from a woman is being fertilized in the laboratory. If successful, the embryo will be implanted in a woman's womb to continue growing naturally.*

## What is in vitro fertilization?

*In vitro fertilization* is commonly known as *IVF*. It is a form of fertility treatment that involves the egg being taken from a woman and fertilized with male sperm in a laboratory. The fertilized egg is then put back in the woman's womb to develop naturally.

### Activity 1

Study the case of Elizabeth Adeney. In pairs, make a list of the points that make her story so controversial.

In May 2009, Elizabeth Adeney became the oldest British woman to have a baby. Elizabeth, aged 66, paid for IVF treatment in the Ukraine using a donor egg and donor sperm. No British clinic was prepared to treat someone of her age. Ms Adeney, a divorcee who runs her own business, hired a live-in nanny and returned to work a few weeks after the birth.

# Who pays for IVF?

Complex medical procedures like this are costly. In 2006, 62-year-old Patricia Rashbrook travelled to Russia for fertility treatment using her 60-year-old husband's sperm and a donor egg. The treatment cost £10,000.

The National Health Service (NHS) knows that many people cannot afford this and couples can have three attempts at IVF treatment without paying, provided:

- the mother is between 23 and 39 at the time of treatment
- at least one partner has been diagnosed with a fertility problem
- at least one partner has been infertile for at least three years.

In the UK, it costs between £4,000 and £8,000 for IVF treatment using the woman's eggs and her partner's sperm. Costs rise when a donor is involved. Because some hospitals are very short of money, not all women are able to get the help they want. Some claim it is a 'postcode lottery'.

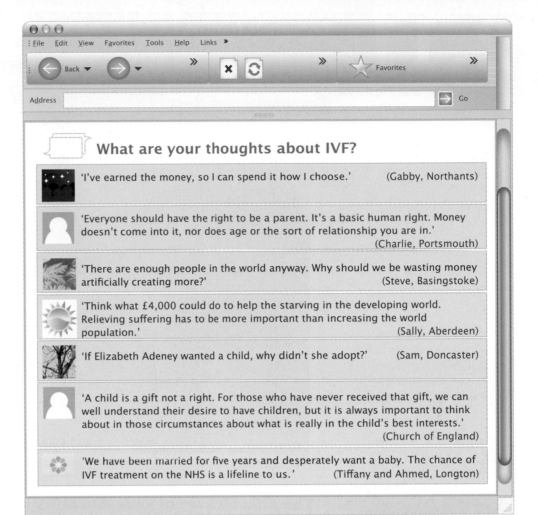

## What are your thoughts about IVF?

'I've earned the money, so I can spend it how I choose.' (Gabby, Northants)

'Everyone should have the right to be a parent. It's a basic human right. Money doesn't come into it, nor does age or the sort of relationship you are in.' (Charlie, Portsmouth)

'There are enough people in the world anyway. Why should we be wasting money artificially creating more?' (Steve, Basingstoke)

'Think what £4,000 could do to help the starving in the developing world. Relieving suffering has to be more important than increasing the world population.' (Sally, Aberdeen)

'If Elizabeth Adeney wanted a child, why didn't she adopt?' (Sam, Doncaster)

'A child is a gift not a right. For those who have never received that gift, we can well understand their desire to have children, but it is always important to think about in those circumstances about what is really in the child's best interests.' (Church of England)

'We have been married for five years and desperately want a baby. The chance of IVF treatment on the NHS is a lifeline to us.' (Tiffany and Ahmed, Longton)

# What do Christians think about IVF?

Christians differ in their attitude towards fertility treatment:

- Some believe a child is a gift from God and humans have no right to interfere with God's plan.
- Others argue that if God gave us the medical knowledge and ability to help infertile couples, we should use it. There are Bible stories of God bringing happiness to an infertile woman by giving her a baby, so IVF is acceptable.
- Some Christians accept IVF if the husband's sperm and wife's egg are used, but not a donor egg or sperm because that is classed as adultery.
- Some Christians do not accept IVF because 'spare' fertilized embryos are destroyed and no human life should ever be destroyed.
- Some Christians do not think the cost of IVF is justified when so many children are starving.

# What do Muslims think about IVF?

IVF is acceptable to many Muslims provided only the egg and sperm from that married couple are used. Anything else is considered to be adultery, and the Qur'an states that sperm should not be wasted. Most Muslims accept the destruction of spare embryos created by IVF because Islam teaches that an embryo only becomes fully human after ensoulment takes place at 120 days.

**Check you have learnt:**

- two arguments in favour of IVF
- two arguments against IVF
- Christian views about IVF
- Muslim views about IVF.

## Activity 2

Try this (c) question:

> God should decide if people should have a baby, not a doctor.

Give **two** reasons why a religious believer might agree or disagree with this statement. (4)

**TRY YOUR SKILL AT THIS**

**The (e) question:**

'Money spent on IVF would be better spent saving life.'

Do you agree? Give reasons or evidence for your answer, showing that you have thought of more than one point of view. You must include reference to religious beliefs in your answer. (8)

In this topic you will think about some real-life problems people have faced concerning medical ethics.

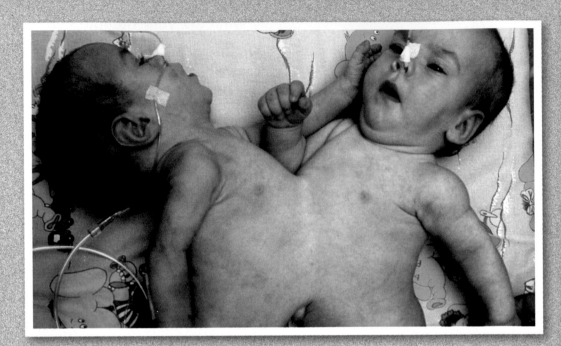

*These are conjoined twins. They have some of their own organs, but also share some between the two of them. Any operation to separate them would involve transplant surgery and may risk the lives of the babies. What religious problems does their treatment raise?*

### The difficult case of Jodie and Mary

Roman Catholics were faced with a difficult ethical dilemma when conjoined twins Jodie and Mary were born to Catholic parents in 2000. Mary, the weaker twin, shared many organs with her twin Jodie. If they were not separated, both twins would die because Jodie's heart and lungs were doing the work for both of them. Doctors wanted to separate the twins and transplant all the organs into Jodie so she would stand a chance of surviving. This would mean the death of Mary.

The twins' parents refused because they said what had happened was God's will and humans should not intervene. They wanted the twins cared for but nature to be allowed to take its course even though surgeons said the twins were unlikely to survive beyond six months. A court case followed and doctors were given permission to go against the parents' wishes and separate the twins, even though it was known one would die.

Alan Dickson, one of the leading surgeons in the team of 22 who did the operation and is a committed Christian, spoke of the moment when they severed Mary's blood supply: 'It was an intense moment. We looked at each other because we knew what we were doing at the time. One doesn't do that kind of thing without having a lot of thought and a lot of heartache. The theatre was very quiet and we treated that moment with the utmost dignity and respect.' Mary died but, after further operations, Jodie has been able to enjoy a normal life.

### Activity 1

Draw **two** columns to show the reasons why some people objected to the separation of Jodie and Mary and others favoured it. What difference did religious beliefs make?

Diane Blood made legal history in 1998 when she gave birth to a baby using her dead husband's sperm. Because the sperm had been taken from her husband when he was in a coma and could not give his consent, its use was illegal under British law. However, the Court of Appeal allowed Mrs Blood to take the sperm to Europe for IVF treatment because it was known her husband had wanted them to start a family.

*RUGBY PLAYER CHOOSES DEATH*

On 18 October 2008, Daniel James (centre) became the youngest person to go to the Dignitas clinic in Switzerland for assisted suicide rather than face a lifetime of pain. Dan, from Worcestershire, was paralysed from the neck downwards after a scrum collapsed on him during rugby training. Previously a robust and very active young man, the 23 year old had no movement in any limbs, was incontinent and in pain. He decided his quality of life was so poor he wanted to end his life. Dan and his parents travelled to Switzerland for an assisted suicide that is illegal in the UK.

In a statement the family said, 'His death was an extremely sad loss for his family, friends and all those who care for him, but no doubt a welcome relief from the 'prison' he felt his body had become'.

## Activity 2

How do you think a religious believer might react to Dan's case? Why?

## Who decides?

In November 2009, the father of a severely disabled baby boy – known as Baby RB – went to court to fight the hospital's attempt to turn off the 13-month-old's life-support machine. The hospital's decision was backed by the baby boy's mother.

Baby RB was incapable of moving his limbs or breathing and swallowing unaided. His father wanted his son to continue receiving hospital care.

## Activity 3

If you were the judge, what sort of evidence would you require to decide on Baby RB's fate?

Look at the BBC news website to find out how this case was resolved.

## Activity 4

Try this (c) question:

> People should be able to choose the sort of baby they have.

Give **two** reasons why a religious believer might agree or disagree with this statement. (4)

### JUDGE RULES WHITE COUPLE CAN KEEP BLACK IVF TWINS AFTER HOSPITAL BLUNDER

### MOTHER OF FIVE GIRLS DEMANDS IVF TO HAVE A SON

# Designer baby

How would you feel if you discovered that your parents had only decided to have you because they wanted to use blood from your umbilical cord to save your brother or sister's life? This is the question Jamie Whitaker will face when he grows up. He was conceived as a result of IVF. Embryos that weren't the right match to save his brother Charlie's life were destroyed. Jamie was the right match and so cells from his umbilical cord were used to save Charlie.

✓ **Check you have learnt:**

- two examples of religious beliefs and medicine coming into conflict.

**TRY YOUR SKILL AT THIS**

**The (b) question:**

Explain how having a religious faith might influence someone's decision about medical ethics. (4)

# SKILLS COACHING 6

## END OF CHAPTER 2 CHECK

☑ ### Check the (a) question

In this topic, *Religion and medicine*, you have learnt these **KEY CONCEPTS**:

- conscience
- free will
- Hippocratic Oath
- medical ethics
- quality of life
- sanctity of life

Create a TRUE or FALSE game based on the meaning of these words. Play it with a partner to check your knowledge.

☑ ### Check the (b) question

This is where you are asked how having a religious faith affects someone's response to an issue. Remind yourself of the Christian and the Muslim responses to these issues, but remember you could answer from a general religious perspective provided you have evidence to support your answer:

- medical ethics
- abortion
- euthanasia
- sanctity of life
- spending money on treatments like IVF

☑ ### Check the (d) question

This question will be asking you to explain the response of two religions, or two traditions within the same religion, to an issue. Make sure you know how Muslims and Christians respond to the issues below and whether some Christians hold different views to others:

- why life is so special
- how religion can affect decisions about medical ethics
- who should make choices that involve abortion
- whether it is ever right to end someone's life.

> **! Tip:**
> If both religions have the same response to an issue, don't say 'they think the same' – you won't get any marks. You need to give details for both religions, e.g. *Christians believe life is special… . Muslims also believe life is special… .*

☑ ### Check the (c) and (e) questions

The (c) question is where you are offered a controversial statement in a speech bubble to comment on. In (c) questions the examiner is asking you to apply what you know about Christian and Muslim attitudes, or religious attitudes in general, to the issues mentioned above with an example and a reason in each case.

The (e) question is giving you a chance to have your say. Obviously, your responses to the issues matter. Rehearse the example you would use and two explanations you would give to support your viewpoint. Consider the view a religious believer would take.

Then revise the example with two explanations the alternative viewpoint might give to argue against you. Once again consider how a religious believer would react to this line of argument.

Here is a typical example of how a question on *Religion and medicine* might be presented on the exam paper. Try answering it in exam conditions in order to check your progress. Remember to use the visual stimuli. Look on page 37 to remind you how these can help.

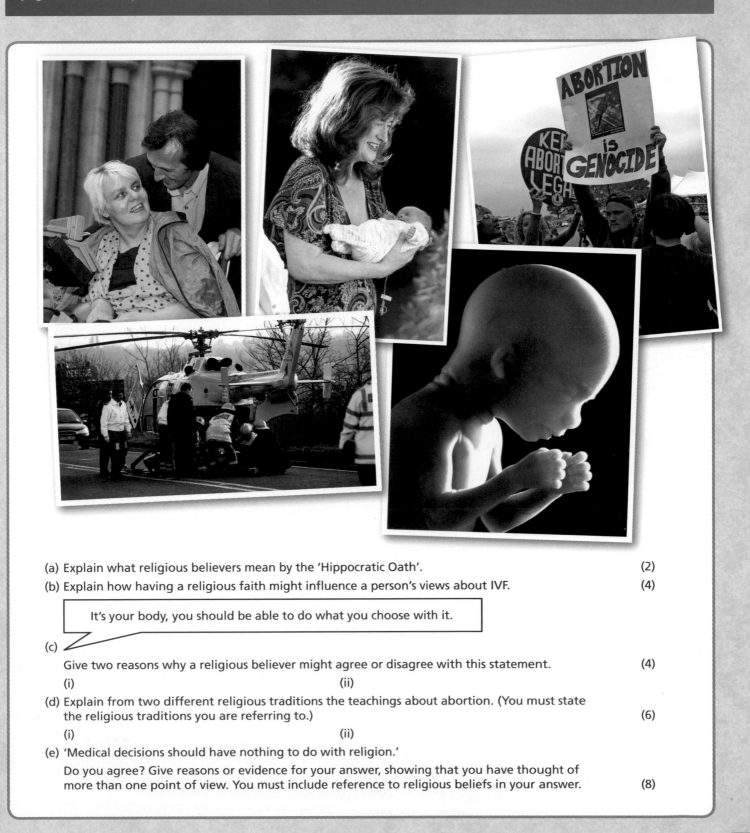

(a) Explain what religious believers mean by the 'Hippocratic Oath'. (2)

(b) Explain how having a religious faith might influence a person's views about IVF. (4)

> It's your body, you should be able to do what you choose with it.

(c)

Give two reasons why a religious believer might agree or disagree with this statement. (4)

(i)                                              (ii)

(d) Explain from two different religious traditions the teachings about abortion. (You must state the religious traditions you are referring to.) (6)

(i)                                              (ii)

(e) 'Medical decisions should have nothing to do with religion.'

Do you agree? Give reasons or evidence for your answer, showing that you have thought of more than one point of view. You must include reference to religious beliefs in your answer. (8)

# CHAPTER 3 Religious expression

CHRIST DIED FOR THE UNGODLY
ROM. 5 v 6

## KEY CONCEPTS KEY C

**community** a group of people who are joined together because they share something in common

**evangelism** spreading a faith or religion to others

**faith** to have trust or confidence

**identity** the sense of who you are in terms of attitudes, character and personality

**pilgrimage** a form of spiritual adventure

**sacred** something to be revered or respected above other things

**In this topic you will think about the different ways in which people express their religious beliefs.**

**community** a group of people who are joined together because they share something in common

**identity** the sense of who you are in terms of attitudes, character and personality

**sacred** something to be revered or respected above other things

## Joining in community worship

Having a religious belief draws many believers together to worship God as a group. Their religion may tell them this is what God requires and they benefit from joining a **community** of fellow believers. Going to a special place of worship can help people to focus on worship. Joining with others who share the same beliefs is not only a powerful spiritual experience, but people can learn more about their religion from their leaders or other worshippers.

## Displaying religious symbols and clothing

Some religious believers like to wear a symbol of their religion – their religion is as much a part of their **identity** as the clothes they choose. They may wear a necklace with a symbol tucked out of sight under a shirt, so they have a private sense that God is always with them. Others choose something very visible. This might be a religious symbol displayed openly around their neck, or special clothing that marks them out as a follower of a certain religion. Not only does this help them to keep their religion at the forefront of their life, but it is also a public declaration of who they are and what they believe in.

## How do people express their religious beliefs?

## Going on a pilgrimage

For some people, having a religious faith is part of their journey through life. The more they learn about their religion, the more they grow in faith. To help their spiritual education, some people go on a journey to **sacred** places associated with their religion. It might be a place where an event in that religion actually happened, or a place that helps worshippers draw closer to God. All pilgrimages play a vital role in the believer's spiritual growth.

## Helping others

Some religious believers choose to express their beliefs by taking action to help others. This could be in a small way by doing something to help a neighbour, or on a larger scale by supporting the work of a religious charity. A believer might give money or take a hands-on approach by working with those in need.

## Activity 1

Try this (c) question:

> Religion is your own business; you should keep it that way.

Give **two** reasons why a religious believer might agree or disagree with this statement. (4)

## Activity 2

Make a poster showing the different ways in which people might express their religious beliefs.

## Private worship

Not all believers choose to express their faith in a public way. For some, religion is a deeply personal matter between them and God. They may express their faith through prayer, reading the scriptures or meditating in a quiet place on their own.

## Missionary work

Some religious believers are convinced that they have a duty to go out and preach the message about their religion to others in order to convert them. This is because they are convinced theirs is the right way and they have a duty to lead others along that path to God.

**Check you have learnt:**

- two ways in which a person might follow their religion privately
- two ways in which a person might follow their religion publicly.

**TRY YOUR SKILL AT THIS**

**The (b) question:**

Explain how having a religious faith might influence a person's behaviour. (4)

# Case study of a Christian organization that is putting its faith into action

In this topic you will find out how the Christian charity CAFOD puts its faith and beliefs into action.

*What does CAFOD's strap line actually mean and what is it telling people about this charity's approach? Think about the word 'just'.*

## Who exactly is CAFOD?

The letters stand for the Catholic Agency for Overseas Development.

They state:

> *"Our mission is to promote human development and social justice in witness to Christian faith and Gospel values."*

## Why does CAFOD do this work?

The reasons they give are:

● all human beings have a right to dignity and respect

● the world's resources are a gift to be shared equally

● all men and women, whatever their race, nationality or religion, have a right to the world's resources

● when confronted by poverty and suffering, compassion is a normal human response.

CAFOD goes on to explain that their Christian motivation is:

● inspired by scriptures

● drawn from the social teachings of the Church

● based on the experiences and hopes of the poor.

### Activity 1

a) What two things do CAFOD set out to do?

b) Explain why poverty causes a problem with each of these aims.

## Expressing Christian beliefs through action

### Activity 2

Try this (c) question:

> Being a believer means you have to do something for the needy.

Give **two** reasons why a religious believer might agree or disagree with this statement. (4)

Because HIV/AIDS is linked to poverty, CAFOD pays for a programme educating people about the spread of this disease. Those being taught can pass the information on to others. AIDS prevention is especially important because it is the main cause of adult death in many poorer countries.

well digging

The provision of clean water and good sanitation is vital for a community's long-term survival. Without clean water, ill health and poverty follow quickly. For this reason, CAFOD is committed to long-term projects such as building wells. As Christians, they believe in helping these communities with long-term projects like building hospitals and schools, as well as setting up farming projects.

CAFOD campaigns against the damage gold-mining operations cause to communities in Honduras and parts of the Congo. They do this because, as Christians, Jesus taught them the importance of helping those who cannot help themselves. Without CAFOD, no one would hear the voices of poor communities who are being exploited by big businesses.

Besides raising money and setting up relief operations, CAFOD knows it is vital to raise public awareness about what is happening. Here, their supporters are marching in support of the 'Make Poverty History' campaign.

Natural disasters hit poor countries most severely and, without immediate help, many people can be plunged into long-term poverty. Here in Haiti, which was hit by four hurricanes in three weeks, CAFOD supplied emergency aid such as drinking water, food, clothes, beds, batteries, blankets, towels, chlorine, mosquito nets and medicines. Their Christian beliefs led them to assist with long-term aid as well, in order to get people back on their feet.

## Activity 3

Design a flyer to go on a church bookstall asking Christians to support one of CAFOD's campaigns. Make sure you tell them what is going on and how this offers them an opportunity to express their faith through action.

✓ **Check you have learnt:**

- the name of one Christian charity
- three things CAFOD does to help people
- three Christian reasons CAFOD gives for its work.

**TRY YOUR SKILL AT THIS**

**The (b) question:**

Explain how having a religious faith might encourage a believer to work for a charity. (4)

In this topic you will find out how the Muslim charity Islamic Relief puts its faith and beliefs into action.

## What exactly is Islamic Relief?

Islamic Relief is an international relief and development charity, which aims to alleviate the suffering of the world's poorest people. As well as responding to disasters and emergencies, Islamic Relief promotes sustainable economic and social development by working with local communities – regardless of race, religion or gender.

## Why does Islamic Relief do this work?

Islamic Relief's vision is of 'a caring world where the basic requirements of people in need are fulfilled.' As Muslims, Islamic Relief workers should put their faith into action by helping everyone in need, no matter who they are. Here are two passages of scripture that inspire the charity's work:

> *Whoever saved a human life shall be regarded as having saved all mankind.*
> **(Qur'an 5:32)**

> *He who goes to sleep on a full stomach while his neighbour goes hungry is not one of us.*
> **(Prophet Muhammad)**

These are some of the things Islamic Relief aims to do:

- Provide assistance regardless of race, colour, politics, gender or religion without expecting anything in return.
- Work to ease the effect of disasters with emergency and long-term aid.
- Promote sustainable development through programmes in education, health and nutrition, water and sanitation, and income generation.
- Speak out on behalf of the poor.

### Activity 1

Both Islamic Relief and CAFOD have taken part in the 'Make Poverty History' marches. Why might they both feel it is their religious duty to campaign? Do you agree with religions getting involved like this? Give your reasons.

# Expressing Muslim beliefs through action

## Campaigning

Muslims believe it is important to let everybody know about the problems that exist in the world. Islamic Relief gives a voice to the poor and those who would normally be overlooked. Like CAFOD on pages 72–73 and Christian Aid, Islamic Relief has joined in the campaign to 'Make Poverty History'.

## Education and training

Without education, people stand little chance of getting out of poverty. Islamic Relief works with communities to find out what they need and set up suitable projects. This might involve supplying a classroom, canteen facilities and food, as well as training teachers. Muslims believe that Allah created all human beings equal and, by supporting projects like this, they are doing what Allah requires.

*Islamic Relief have set up a bread oven to help people earn a living.*

## Income generation

Poor people want to work so they can support themselves. Islamic Relief sets up all sorts of training programmes, from computing to making handicrafts, to helping farmers with seeds and fertilizers. The charity can also help with small interest-free loans to help people start their own business.

## Orphan sponsorship

Children who have lost parents and have been left to struggle alone desperately need help. Islamic Relief sponsors over 26,000 children, providing them with shelter, healthcare and education. Because Prophet Muhammad was an orphan, Muslims understand how vital it is to help children who have no one to turn to.

## Emergency relief

Islamic Relief is always prepared to supply an effective emergency response for any disaster. The charity immediately provides food, medicine and temporary shelter as it works out what the best long-term help for that community will be. This is one way in which Muslims can help to relieve suffering.

## Water and sanitation

If people don't have adequate water and sanitation, they get sick and die. Water shortages also lead to crop failures and starvation. Islamic Relief builds water supply systems, digs wells, and sets up water purification and sanitation projects.

## Health and nutrition

When people don't get enough to eat, they become ill and die. Islamic Relief provides healthcare for everyone in need. This can be everything from a clinic, to nurses, equipment and drugs, alongside educating people about health and diet. The words of Prophet Muhammad on the opposite page explain why Muslims believe this is an important way of putting their faith into practice.

*Providing a supply of fresh drinking water will save countless lives.*

---

## Activity 2

Try this (c) question:

> Religious believers shouldn't campaign on the streets.

Give **two** reasons why a religious believer might agree or disagree with this statement. (4)

## Activity 3

Choose **one** of the areas featured on these pages and go to www.islamic-relief.org.uk to find out more details about the charity's actions.

### ✓ Check you have learnt:

- the name of one Muslim charity
- three things Islamic Relief does to help people
- the religious reasons for Islamic Relief's work.

### TRY YOUR SKILL AT THIS

**The (d) question:**

Explain how **two** different religious organizations or charities express their faith through their work. (You must state the religious traditions you are referring to.) (6)

### Improve your skill with the (a) question

Check you know the meaning of the **KEY CONCEPTS** that have appeared in this topic so far:

- community (page 70)
- identity (page 70)
- sacred (page 70)

Try writing out the meaning for each key concept, then check your answers.

### Improve your skill with the (b) question

Making use of the step-by-step approach you have learnt already, choose one of the (b) questions below to answer.

Remember: **POINT + EXAMPLE + EXPLANATION**

Make a special effort to make accurate use of some specialist language in your answer.

Explain how having a religious faith might lead some people to express their faith through action. (4)

Explain how having a religious faith might lead some people to express their faith in a private way. (4)

### Improve your skill with the (d) question

The sort of issues you should revise for a (d) question on the work you have done so far in *Religious expression* are:

- the ways Muslims and Christians express their beliefs
- case studies of the ways Muslims and Christians put their faith into action.

Use the step-by-step method (on page 56) to plan out an answer to each one. Look at the stimulus on pages 68–69 and see if it will help you. Plan to include some specialist language in your answer.

Chan was faced with this question:

Explain from two different religious traditions how people might put their faith into action. (6)

He wrote:

> Muslims can do lots of things to show they believe in Allah. They pray five times a day and read the Qur'an. Most Muslim women cover their heads because that is what the Qur'an says they should do. Some Muslims give money to charities like Islamic Relief or Muslim Aid to help the poor.
>
> Christians can go on pilgrimage to places like Bethlehem where Jesus was born so they can get closer to God. They can also give money to Christian Aid or volunteer to help a charity. This shows they are doing what their religion wants them to do.

Grade Chan's answer using the mark scheme on page 24. Don't forget to check his use of specialist language. What helpful comments would you write at the bottom of Chan's answer? Look on page 128 to see what the examiner had to say about Chan's answer.

**Tip:**
Don't fall into the trap of thinking that if you write lots about one religion you can get lots of marks. It doesn't work like that! The examiner is considering your overall level of understanding of the issue under discussion, so try to analyse both religions in the same amount of detail.

# WHAT DO PEOPLE THINK?

## Improve your skill with the (c) and (e) questions

Both the (c) and the (e) questions start off with a statement from everyday life.
Sonja tackled the following (c) question:

> Religious people should get involved with charity work.

Give two reasons why a religious believer might agree or disagree with this statement.    (4)

Her teacher encouraged her to aim higher with her answer and so she decided to explain how someone in the religion might be able to agree and disagree. Sonja thought this would show she had a really good understanding of the teachings.

> Religious people ought to get involved in helping the poor because this is what their scriptures teach, and many holy people in the past helped people. Muhammad did.
> But, on the other hand, it might be better if they gave money to a television appeal. The organizations know what they are doing and they are ready to send teams of experts at a moment's notice. Christian Aid has got years of experience in disaster relief and it can target the right places.

**Be the examiner:** Read what Sonja has written and compare it with the mark scheme on page 25. Look to see where Sonja has given an example and explained it each time. What mark do you think she has earned and why? If she asked you about getting a higher mark, what advice would you give? Look on page 128 to see what the examiner had to say.

If this same statement had turned up as an (e) question, you would have been able to give your opinion. Write a paragraph saying whether you agree or disagree with the statement Sonja tackled. Give an example and explain it. When examiners are marking an (e) question, they are looking out for the use of specialist language. Did Sonja have any in her answer? What could you include in yours to access the higher marks?

Look at the way Josh tackled this (e) question and what the examiner thought of it.

> 'Religious people should leave charity work to the experts.'

> Do you agree? Give reasons or evidence for your answer, showing that you have thought of more than one point of view. You must include reference to religious beliefs in your answer.    (8)

> A lot of people who are religious do get involved in charity work and some probably do more harm than good because they don't really know what is needed. A Christian might say that it is better to give money to a proper charity that has people trained for the job than make a bungled effort. I have heard about people collecting loads of clothes for some earthquake victims and sending a lorry out there, but the clothes were all wrong for that sort of climate and culture. It was a real waste of money. It would have been much better if they had given money to a charity that knows all about these things.
> Then again, other religious people point out that most charities began life because religious people did care and took no notice of others and just got stuck in. Islamic Relief started that way when a Muslim student was determined to help people dying in the Sudan. If he hadn't taken action, then many more would have died.

The examiner said:

Josh's answer is good. He has offered two different points of view and used specialist language well. This is not a top-level answer because he has not discussed each side of the argument thoroughly enough so I would award him Level 3 and 6 marks.

Copy Josh's answer on to your page. Use the **Point + example + explanation + religious explanation** method you learnt on page 57 to analyse each paragraph. Underline in colour where you think the points, examples and explanations are. Can you develop the argument in each paragraph one stage further to access the highest level?

## Why do some Christians choose to wear special clothes?

In this topic you will explore how some Christians express their faith through what they wear.

**faith** to have trust or confidence

*Useful specialist language*

**symbol** to represent an idea through an image or action

*The Archbishop of York is wearing robes that display many symbols of his Christian faith.*

## Activity 1

Find out what the symbols on the archbishop's robes tell us about his Christian beliefs:

- the cross with beams of light coming from it
- the Alpha and Omega sign in the centre of his mitre (hat)
- the tongues of fire design on his shoulder
- the cross with a figure on it, around the archbishop's neck
- the white lamb just showing on the right-hand side of his robe.

## Christians and symbols

There is no religious obligation for most Christians to wear special clothing in their daily life or in their worship. However, some Christians choose to display religious **symbols** on their person or around them. It is not unusual to see a fish symbol on the back of a car or a cross displayed on a mantelpiece in the home. Both show that the person is a Christian. It is usual for a religious leader, like the Archbishop of York, to wear special clothes and symbols during a ceremony so worshippers know who their leader is.

# Why display symbols?

You might think it is unlikely that someone is going to forget what religion they belong to. This is true, but some Christians say that having a religious symbol around them helps them to keep God in the forefront of their mind. For others, displaying a symbol is also a way of advertising their religion to others. This might lead somebody who sees the symbol to become interested enough in the religion to find out more and join it.

*This Christian belongs to a denomination called the Salvation Army. Wearing a uniform is an important part of their faith.*

For some Christians, like members of the Salvation Army, their clothing is an important part of who they are and what they stand for. Salvationists wear a dark-coloured uniform that looks like a military uniform. It symbolizes that they are soldiers of Christ who fight against the evils in the world.

## Activity 2

List all the reasons why Christians choose to wear special garments or symbols of their faith.

## Activity 3

Go to the BBC News website to find out more about British Airways check-in worker, Nadia Eweida, and her fight to be allowed to wear a cross necklace as a symbol of her faith.

## The robes of authority

Most leaders in the Christian religion wear special garments. This enables followers to have **faith** in their leaders' judgment. For some denominations, like Methodists, their leaders just wear a 'dog collar' – a white band under the collar of their shirt. Other priests dress in more elaborate robes and the highest leaders of the denomination, like the Pope or the archbishops, have very ornate robes.

Priests are required to wear robes when they conduct ceremonies. This is because wearing special robes helps members of the faith to identify who is in authority amongst them. More significantly, by taking the trouble to dress in a particular way with richly-decorated garments, the wearer is showing the importance of the role they play in the ceremony. A priest wears his full robes when he takes the Communion service, to show respect for Jesus and help the members of the congregation feel the holiness of the occasion.

✔ **Check you have learnt:**

- the Christian attitude towards religious dress
- two reasons why some Christians wear religious garments
- two symbols that Christians might wear.

**TRY YOUR SKILL AT THIS**

**The (e) question:**

'Faith is a personal thing; no one has the right to tell you what to wear.'

Do you agree? Give reasons or evidence for your answer, showing that you have thought of more than one point of view. You must include reference to religious beliefs in your answer. (8)

## Activity 4

Try this (c) question:

> It's what is in your heart that matters, not what you wear.

Give **two** reasons why a religious believer might agree or disagree with this statement. (4)

## Activity 5

As a group, discuss what, if any, rules there should be about the wearing of religious symbols or clothing at school. Should people who work at a school have more, or less, freedom than students? Why?

## Why do some Muslims choose to wear special clothes?

**In this topic you will examine the reasons why some Muslims express their faith through what they wear.**

Many Muslims show their outward commitment to their religion through the clothes they wear, but Islam does not insist on particular garments being worn. What the Qur'an does tell Muslims is that they must behave and dress modestly. This means that wearing revealing or clingy clothes goes against the teachings of Islam.

> I am not forced to cover my head; I do it because I choose to. I feel more comfortable when I am dressed modestly. I want people to see me for the person I am inside, not make judgements about my sex appeal or my looks. Being a Muslim is an important part of my identity; I am happy for others to know that.

### Activity 1

Write a letter from a Muslim parent to the secondary school their daughter is moving to. Explain why it is important that she is allowed to adapt the school uniform to suit the requirement for modesty in her religion.

Rules about modest clothing apply to men just as much as to women. A Muslim man is required to dress himself modestly and ensure he is covered from his navel to his knees. Modest dressing for many Muslim women means covering themselves from their wrists to their ankles, in addition to covering their hair. This is a symbol that they want to keep themselves pure.

# Dressing for prayer

For Muslims, prayer is an important part of their daily life. It is the second pillar of Islam and they are required to pray five times a day. Preparation for prayer not only requires a ritual wash, called wudu, but also requires a Muslim to make sure that they are dressed properly. When a Muslim goes before Allah in prayer, they should be dressed modestly with their head covered, even if they do not normally cover their head. Clothes must be clean. By taking special care with their appearance, a Muslim is showing Allah how important he is to them. The act of checking the clothing before prayer, like the ritual washing, helps a Muslim to focus their mind on the importance of the actions they are about to begin. Taking care with their appearance makes them fully aware that they are in the presence of Allah.

# Dressing for pilgrimage

When Muslims go on the pilgrimage to Makkah, called hajj, they put on special clothing (ihram). It symbolizes that all Muslims are equal and reminds believers of the need to keep themselves pure in mind and body during the pilgrimage. These simple pieces of white cotton sheet can be seen being worn on hajj in the picture below and on page 90.

October 2004

## FRANCE BANS RELIGIOUS SYMBOLS IN SCHOOL

There was an outcry when the French government introduced a law banning all religious symbols from its schools. This is part of the French government's move to take all forms of religion out of schools. No religious symbols, like the crucifix, can be displayed on a classroom wall and no one can wear religious clothing. It means Sikhs cannot wear the turban nor Muslim girls the hijab. A spokesman for the government said they wanted to keep the state and religion totally separate. Those who are against this move say it is an infringement of a person's human rights.

---

**Activity 2**

List all the reasons given on these pages for Muslims choosing to wear particular garments to express their faith. Is there any difference between a Muslim's reasons for wearing religious garments and those of a Christian monk or nun?

**Activity 3**

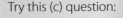

Try this (c) question:

> Schools should allow students to wear religious clothing.

Give **two** reasons why a religious believer might agree or disagree with this statement. (4)

✓ **Check you have learnt:**

- how Muslims are required to dress according to the Qur'an
- why many Muslim women cover their hair
- how Muslims dress for prayer and why.

**TRY YOUR SKILL AT THIS**

**The (e) question:**

'True religion has got nothing to do with clothes; it's all a big fuss about nothing.'

Do you agree? Give reasons or evidence for your answer, showing that you have thought of more than one point of view. You must include reference to religious beliefs in your answer. (8)

# 3.6

## How do Christians use symbolism in their place of worship?

In this topic you will study the Christian attitude to art and symbolism in their worship.

Christians vary in their attitude to symbolism in worship. A few, like Quakers, prefer everything to be plain and simple. For them, worship is what goes on between God and a person's mind, the place doesn't matter. It can be anywhere, outside or inside, without special preparations. Indeed, some would say special pictures, symbols and clothing are a distraction rather than a help.

Orthodox Christians take a totally different view. They believe that a place of worship should be richly decorated to show humans are offering the very best they can to God. The pictures, statues and decorations in their churches help worshippers get into the right frame of mind to come before God. Pictures and statues provide the worshipper with something to meditate on.

## Activity 1

Try this (c) question:

> Religious paintings are a distraction.

Give **two** reasons why a religious believer might agree or disagree with this statement. (4)

# Some of the features that might appear in a Christian place of worship

### Pulpit and lectern

In some Christian places of worship the pulpit, where the preacher stands, and the lectern, where the Bible is read, are very prominent. This is to symbolize the importance of the Word of God in Christian life, whether it is read to them or explained to them by the preacher.

### The altar

In most churches, the altar is the focal point of the building. This reminds Christians of the table where Jesus ate his last supper and where Christians today can share Holy Communion to remember Jesus.

### The cross

The cross is the most important symbol for Christians because it reminds them that Jesus gave his life to save people from sin, and gave them everlasting life. Many Christians use this symbol to meditate on the sacrifice Jesus made for them.

### Stained-glass windows

The stained-glass windows usually contain pictures of biblical stories or scenes from the lives of saints. These pictures help to remind Christians of important events and people in their past, and they might inspire the worshipper to take action.

### Statues and images

Some Christians find that praying in front of an image helps them to focus on the person it represents. No Christian worships a statue; it is the person the plaster image represents on which the Christian is concentrating. Mary, the mother of Christ, is a popular statue in Catholic churches and helps Christians to focus on virtues like love and humility. Some Christians may choose to pray to the person shown in the statue and ask them to talk to God on their behalf.

*The simplicity of this chapel in Wales contrasts sharply with the ornate splendour of the Greek Orthodox Church opposite, yet both assist Christian worship.*

## Worshipping together

Private prayer is important for Christians, but joining others in worship is equally significant; some would say it is more important. Jesus told his followers:

> *For where two or three come together in my name, I am there with them.*
> **(Matthew 18:20)**

Many Christians feel they can make contact with God or Jesus better if they are surrounded by other Christians in a place of worship, rather than at home on their own.

Being surrounded by symbols of their faith or pictures helps to focus the Christian's mind on God. The darkness of some churches and the smell of incense can help people to settle into an atmosphere of worship. Others may find these things a distraction and question whether money spent on religious works of art wouldn't be better spent helping the needy in God's world.

Worshipping in a special place also has the advantage of putting the Christian in touch with their religious leader who can help them with practical and religious issues.

---

## Activity 2

List **four** reasons why a Christian might prefer to worship in a church rather than at home.

---

✔ **Check you have learnt:**

- how some Christians use artwork in their place of worship
- two reasons why Christians worship in a church
- two symbols a Christian might find helpful in worship.

---

**TRY YOUR SKILL AT THIS**

**The (e) question:**

'Money should be spent helping people, not decorating a place of worship.'

Do you agree? Give reasons or evidence for your answer, showing that you have thought of more than one point of view. You must include reference to religious beliefs in your answer. (8)

**In this topic you will study the Muslim attitude to art and symbolism in their worship.**

*Useful specialist language*

**ummah** the feeling of brotherhood amongst all Muslims

Prayer is a very important part of daily life for a Muslim. Because they are required to pray five times a day, prayer can take place anywhere provided the place is clean and enables the worshipper to focus fully on Allah. Symbols or special furniture are unnecessary.

The Qur'an teaches Muslims that it is wrong to attempt to make any image of Allah. No human can possibly know what Allah is like, so it is disrespectful to attempt it. Because Muslims believe that only Allah can create a human being, it is also wrong for them to draw pictures of people. This means that when a Muslim prays at home, or at the mosque, there will not be any pictures of people around them.

This does not mean that a mosque, or the home, is completely bare. There are likely to be various symbols around that help worshippers focus their thoughts on Allah. This might take the form of writings from the Qur'an or pictures of the holy city of Makkah. Mosques can be very beautiful places of worship. Their decoration comes not from statues or paintings, but from geometric patterns. The colourful and intricate patterns never contain images of people or animals, but their rich colours and designs are beautiful offerings to Allah and can help a Muslim to focus on Allah.

## Calligraphy

Words from the Qur'an can often be seen on the walls in the mosque, written in the most beautiful Arabic calligraphy. Not only do they decorate the building, more importantly, they are there so Muslims can read and meditate on the Word of Allah.

The only pictures that might adorn the mosque are likely to be photographs or pieces of artwork showing the prophet's mosque at Makkah, where Muslims go on hajj (pilgrimage), or the holy city of Medina where Prophet Muhammad is buried.

## The mihrab

Muslims pray facing the holy city of Makkah. The right direction is shown in the mosque by the mihrab, which is an alcove. Some say the shape of the alcove symbolizes the ear of Allah being always open to the prayers of Muslims.

## The prayer mat

The mat a Muslim uses for prayer also contains important religious symbols. Although designs and colours vary, the rug will always have an arch representing the mihrab in the mosque to show a Muslim they are facing Makkah. A lamp can often be seen hanging from the arch, and flowers and plants are shown near the base of the arch.

The prayer mat reminds a Muslim of the need to pray five times a day and to find a clean place to pray in.

In a mosque, the carpet is designed to look like individual prayer mats.

*This detail is from the mosque known as the Dome of the Rock, the third most holy site in Islam. Its beauty comes from the use of colour and geometric patterns.*

## Worshipping together

Muslims are taught that joining with others for prayer pleases Allah and many men try to come together for Friday prayers at the mosque. Joining others in worship strengthens the feeling of **ummah** and enables Muslims to listen to their religious leader preach the Friday sermon. All of this can help to strengthen a person's faith.

**Check you have learnt:**

- why Muslims do not have pictures of people in their places of worship
- two symbols a Muslim might find helpful in worship.

### Activity 1

Explain why a Muslim would want to see symbols not drawings of people in their place of worship.

### Activity 2

Try this (c) question:

> Places of worship need plenty of religious symbols to help a believer pray.

Give **two** reasons why a religious believer might agree or disagree with this statement. (4)

**TRY YOUR SKILL AT THIS**

**The (d) question:**

Explain from **two** different religious traditions how members of the faith make their place of worship helpful to prayer. (You must state the religious traditions you are referring to.) (6)

## DO YOU UNDERSTAND?

### Improve your skill with the (a) question

| Key concept meanings | Key concept | Mark |
|---|---|---|
| Something to be revered or respected above other things | | |
| To have trust or confidence | | |
| The sense of who you are in terms of attitudes, character and personality | | |
| A group of people who are joined together because they share something in common | | |

**✳ TRY THIS ✳**

Copy out each of the key concept meanings. Write the correct key concept alongside. Then check your answers against the definitions on page 69.

### Improve your skill with the (b) question

This is the question that is asking you to **make a link** between what a religion teaches and the way a believer behaves.

> **Explain how having a religious faith might lead a believer to wear special clothes.** (4)

Read the question, concentrating on the piece of information at the end of it. Ask yourself a few quick questions to get the ideas flowing.

- What special clothes do religious believers wear?
- When do they wear them?
- Do all, or some, believers wear these garments?

This might lead you to think about how special clothes can be an expression of religion for some people.

What religious language are you going to use in your answer? Think about the names of some religious symbols or clothes you could include. Is there anything in the stimulus to help you?

Here is the answer Ahmed began. Look at the mark scheme on page 24 to see what marks he might get, then copy down what he has written and finish it off to gain 4 marks. Or, if you prefer, change the example and complete the answer.

> *Religious clothes help people to feel closer to God like when a Muslim puts on a hat to do his prayers. That's because ...*

**Tip:**

When you have read the question, look across at the stimulus material to see if there are any helpful ideas there. For instance on page 83 there is a picture of a Welsh chapel. How might that help you to answer the following question?

**Explain how having a religious faith might lead a person to pray in a church. (4)**

### Improve your skill with the (d) question

Remember you will be asked about the way two different religious traditions react to an issue. Based on the most recent work you have done, it is worth drafting out some revision notes on the way both Christians and Muslims express their religion by what they do and what they wear. Because two different religious traditions could also come from within one religion, spend a few moments considering whether there are different views amongst Muslims or Christians on these issues. Write down at least three specialist terms that you could include in an answer.

# WHAT DO PEOPLE THINK?

## Improve your skill with the (e) question

This is the question that is asking for your opinion on a subject and since no one's opinion counts for much unless they can back it up, your answer requires an example and at least two explanations.

Most of the statements you are likely to see in the (e) question will usually relate to everyday life and not a particular religious issue. That's because religion is about life! Real life!

The issues are likely to be ones that you have discussed in class and you have no doubt discovered people in your group hold various different views about the issues. Good! It's worth thinking back to what might have been said because it can supply you with different arguments to use in your answer.

The types of general life issues the examiner may well ask you about on the material you have studied so far in Chapter 3 *Religious expression* are:

- How can art express a person's faith?
- Why do people choose to worship in special buildings?
- Why does religion prompt some people to help others?
- Can religion give people a purpose in life?

Take one of the topics from the list above and jot down some points that could go in an answer. If you think in terms of 'some people do' and 'some people don't' you can see the two possible lines of argument an (e) question could follow. Put down some specialist language you could include in the topic you have chosen. Go back to your list and add examples you could use. What explanations would you give? Check you have got some religious teachings included on your page.

### What is QWC?

**Q**uality of **W**ritten **C**ommunication is where the examiner is rewarding the overall quality of your written English. When the examiners are marking the (e) question they will naturally be concentrating on what you have to say but they will also be paying attention to the way that you say it when they award the marks. These are the things they will be looking out for:

- Is the handwriting legible?
- Is the spelling, punctuation and grammar accurate?

When all these things are weighed up together, the examiner is asking if your written work is communicating clearly.

Whilst you should be aiming for these things all the way through your exam answers, it is when the examiner is marking your (e) answers that it really counts towards your final total. So make sure you leave yourself some checking time at the end of the exam and, if you don't manage anything else, check those (e) questions through very carefully. Remember 8 marks are at stake on every one. That is a lot of marks!

Here is an (e) question for you to try it all out on:

'Religion is about getting out and doing something, not bowing and lighting candles.'

Do you agree? Give reasons for your answer, showing that you have thought of more than one point of view. You must include reference to religious beliefs in your answer.

(8)

## How can Christians express their faith through pilgrimage?

In this topic you will look at the ways some Christians express their faith through pilgrimage.

### KEY CONCEPTS KEY C

**pilgrimage** a form of spiritual adventure

## Why do Christians go on pilgrimage?

It isn't necessary for Christians to make a **pilgrimage** to any sacred place, yet for some this sort of journey is an expression of their faith. There are many places around the world that have religious associations for Christians. Many pilgrimage sites are in Israel where Jesus actually walked and preached. However, there are other places where holy people have lived and worked, and sites where miracles are said to have taken place. Making the effort to travel to a holy site enables some Christians to show God how much they love him, and it helps their own spiritual growth.

## Lourdes

Paul travelled to Lourdes in France with members of the Catholic church that he attends when he was home from university. He says:

### Activity 1

Make a list of the things Paul says he and others gained from a pilgrimage to Lourdes.

"I didn't want to be just another tourist taking photographs of the holy sites and having a holiday, so, I volunteered to be a helper for a month, assisting sick people who come to Lourdes every day. Anyone over 16 can offer their services for a week or longer. Pushing the special blue wheelchairs, helping with shopping, assisting with travel and carrying bags are all part of the job. One of the girls I met was acting as an interpreter for a disabled lady. We wore special uniforms so everyone was clear who we are and what we are doing.

For me, this pilgrimage was a very profound experience. I met some wonderful people who were desperately sick, but filled with great joy and optimism. No, they weren't expecting a miracle cure or anything like that. They came to draw spiritual strength from being near God in a special place and to join so many believers in prayer.

And me? Well, it was the most profoundly moving experience I have ever had in my life. Such love and kindness from people whom I had never met before and such a strong belief in God! I am pleased I went as a pilgrim and not a tourist because it made me feel more involved in things. I think I got more out of it for that reason.

The priest who led our party reminded us that this pilgrimage was a chance for us to use our talents, no matter what they are, to help others. And, although I don't have any medical skills, I did feel I had the chance to help others by being cheerful and willing to do whatever the sick person asked of me – yes, even carrying their handbag! The Lourdes experience is a bit like the journey through life. You are not on your own and it is important to do what you can for those who are travelling with you. After all, we are all travelling towards God; well, that's how I see it."

# The Holy Land

For many Christians, the Holy Land is the only place they want to make a pilgrimage to. This is because they feel closer to Jesus when they are following in his actual footsteps. Some Christians draw strength from being in a group of believers, praying at the sites where Jesus is likely to have prayed.

For others, pilgrimage is a personal journey, taken quietly away from the crowds. They might stop to read passages from the Gospels about what Jesus did at the sacred place, and then they might pray there. For them, all the effort of saving up the money and arranging the travel is an expression of their faith because a pilgrimage can bring them spiritually closer to God.

## Activity 2

Research the pilgrimage site of Walsingham in Norfolk to find out what Christians do when they visit this holy place. An interesting and unusual angle on this topic would be to find out about the different practices of the Russian Orthodox Christians, the Anglicans and the Roman Catholics at their shrines at Walsingham.

*Jerusalem, the holy city where Jesus spent the final days of his life, is an important pilgrimage site for Christians (and also Muslims). This is the garden where Jesus was arrested. Many Christians feel close to Jesus here.*

## Activity 3

Try this (c) question:

> Pilgrimages are unnecessary.

Give **two** reasons why a religious believer might agree or disagree with this statement. (4)

*Many Christians are drawn to pray at this church on the edge of Lake Galilee because Jesus spent most of his life in this area.*

### Check you have learnt:

- the names of two Christian pilgrimage sites
- three ways pilgrimages might help a Christian's spiritual growth
- how faith can be expressed through pilgrimage.

### TRY YOUR SKILL AT THIS

**The (e) question:**

'A pilgrimage is just another name for a holiday.'

Do you agree? Give reasons or evidence for your answer, showing that you have thought of more than one point of view. You must include reference to religious beliefs in your answer. (8)

## What do Muslims gain from pilgrimage?

In this topic you will look at the importance the pilgrimage to Makkah has in a Muslim's spiritual growth.

### Useful specialist language

**hajj** the pilgrimage to Makkah, the fifth pillar of Islam

**ihram** white sheets worn by Muslims on hajj

**umrah** the lesser pilgrimage to Makkah, which can be undertaken at any time of the year

## Hajj

Muslims believe that Allah wants them to go on pilgrimage to Makkah at least once in their lifetime. **Hajj**, the pilgrimage to Makkah, is one of the five pillars of Islam and all who can afford it and are fit enough should try to go. Hajj takes place during one particular month each year, which brings together two to three million Muslims in one place with the sole intention of worshipping Allah. This is a very powerful religious experience! Taking time out of daily life to concentrate totally on the spiritual strengthens most Muslims' faith.

To show how special this religious experience is, Muslims change into **ihram**. For men, this is made up of three white pieces of cotton fabric without seams, for women, five pieces of fabric. Ihram symbolizes purity and humility before Allah. Everyone looks equal when they dress in ihram, no matter whether they are rich or poor. This reminds Muslims that they are all equal in the eyes of Allah and will be treated equally when they come before Allah on the Day of Judgement.

*Muslims express their faith by wearing special clothes on pilgrimage. These clothes are called ihram.*

Pilgrims begin by walking around the Ka'bah, the site of the first place of worship, which stands in the middle of the Great Mosque at Makkah. After circling the Ka'bah seven times, pilgrims begin a set trail that will take them several miles around the holy sites. The route is long and challenging, so completing it for Allah is a great achievement for a Muslim.

At certain points on their journey, Muslims perform rituals with special meanings. They throw pebbles at three stone pillars, to remind them of the need to battle with the devil. They drink water from the well of Zamzam, to remember that Allah will provide all that is needed for them as he did for others in ancient times. For some, the most powerful part of hajj is when they join others on Mount Arafat to pray to Allah on the very spot where Muhammad preached his last sermon. A final important act is the cutting of their hair as a sign of symbolic purity. (In actual fact, the men have their heads shaved, the women just have a lock cut off.)

### Activity 1

Find out what Muslims are reminded of when they run along the passageway called Marwah and Safah, and when an animal is sacrificed at Mina.

## On their return

For most Muslims, this is such an intensely spiritual experience that they feel that their life has changed. Some choose to add the name Hajji as part of their name to symbolize their religious transformation and many become more focused on their religion as a result, making sure they carry out their religious duties with more zeal.

Suma went to Makkah at a different time of the year to hajj; this sort of pilgrimage is called **umrah**.

I travelled to Makkah in November during Ramadan. It took weeks of preparation to ensure I knew the procedures of performing umrah properly, as I wanted to be confident I knew what I was doing.

When I arrived at the mosque, it was nothing like I expected. I thought I'd be driven to a place where the Ka'bah would be right in front of me. But when I arrived I saw lots of people rushing to do their prayers. Once I entered into the mosque, there before my eyes was the Ka'bah. This was the most magical moment in my life. I had shivers down my spine, I started crying. I was crying because for the first time in my life I felt contentment, peace and a sense of belonging. All my troubles seemed so far away and I truly knew what it meant to feel one with Allah.

As I write this, I can hear the sounds of the birds flying around the Ka'bah and the rush of people praying and circling the Ka'bah. I honestly believe that this is where it is all happening. If anyone has any doubts about being a Muslim or what Islam is all about then the holy city is where all the answers are. It feels as though Islam is alive and not just a religion by history, although there is so much to learn. It changed my life.

The experience affects your mind, body and soul. It is physically very challenging as you have so much to do. You have to give up your worldly comforts and therefore it requires willpower and determination.

## Activity 2

Script a radio interview with Suma during which the presenter asks about how Suma's faith was affected by going on pilgrimage.

## Activity 3

Try this (c) question:

> Pilgrimage is the best way to show your faith in God.

Give **two** reasons why a religious believer might agree or disagree with this statement. (4)

**Check you have learnt:**

- why Muslims go on hajj
- three things a Muslim does on hajj
- ways hajj might strengthen a Muslim's faith.

**TRY YOUR SKILL AT THIS**

**The (d) question:**

Explain from **two** different religious traditions why pilgrimage could strengthen a believer's faith. (You must state the religious traditions you are referring to.) (6)

**Hint:** Use these pages along with pages 88–89 to answer from the Christian and Muslim traditions.

## Sharing faith

**In this topic you will examine the way in which one interfaith organization helps people to share their faith.**

*Useful specialist language*

**interfaith** when two or more religions work together in harmony

Here is a case study of one **interfaith** organization that helps believers to share their faith in Bradford and promote community cohesion.

### Bradford District Faiths Forum aims to:

Promote understanding, communication, co-operation and good relations by encouraging faith communities to meet and work together to address issues of shared concern • Advance public knowledge and understanding of the District's different faith communities, including awareness of their distinctive teachings, traditions, practices and of the common ground between them, to promote good community relations • Promote social inclusion and combat religious discrimination by encouraging communication, understanding and partnership between faith communities and with public, voluntary and private sector bodies.

You can see from the aims of this group that community cohesion is at the heart of its activities. Their development coordinator, Nasar Fiaz, says, "I hear many young people say 'the only people I know from another faith were at school with me – and that was years ago.' A clear gap opens between people once they leave school, leaving no scope for independent learning about each other's faiths and cultures."

### Activity 1

Explain how a walk like this could develop feelings of peace and reconciliation in a multi-faith community.

For the past six years a large group of people of all faiths have got together for a Walk of Friendship. They set off from Keighley Town Hall Square (not far from Bradford) and visit various places of worship on the way. They are seen here leaving their first destination, which is the Shah Jalal Mosque. They were welcomed with a tour of the building and listened to poetry recited by young people. Their next destination was the Keighley Shared Church, which had been the Anglican parish church and is now shared with the Methodists' congregation. A further stage of the walk includes a multicultural concert with singing, recitations from the Qur'an and African drumming.

Twenty people from Bradford who represented Christians, Hindus, Sikhs and Muslims got together to plant 100 young trees in the Yorkshire Dales. It was part of a project called Faith in the Environment and aimed 'to put something back into our beautiful environment as well as raise awareness of the scenic beauty on our doorsteps'. The organizers said, "It also highlighted similarities between faiths, rather than their differences."

## Activity 2

a) What are the 'similarities between faiths' that the tree planting project highlighted?

b) Active projects like this are usually extremely successful in getting the faiths to work well together. Why do you think this is?

One hundred and twenty Bradford people representing seven different religions got together to share a meal in a restaurant and discuss the different ways in which they celebrate their festivals. In the picture there are: a Jew; the Dean of Bradford Cathedral; a Muslim; a Hindu; a Sikh; a Buddhist; a Baha'i; and the Bishop of Bradford. The event was so enjoyable it has become an annual one. Nasar said, "The overwhelming message that came across was that different faiths have a lot in common in how they celebrate their festivals. We wear our best clothes, offer prayers, meet family and friends and give, or receive, presents. There was a genuine sense of mutuality and understanding between the people who attended the inaugural event. Everyone appreciated the opportunity to meet others from different faiths and share their rich cultures." A total of £270 was also collected for the Bangladesh Cyclone Appeal.

## Activity 3

Try this (c) question:

> Religions cause wars. They can't possibly work together.

Give **two** reasons why a religious believer might agree or disagree with this statement. (4)

✓ **Check you have learnt:**

- three ways in which religions have worked together
- what they have gained from working together.

**TRY YOUR SKILL AT THIS**

**The (b) question:**

Explain how having a religious faith might encourage a person to take part in an interfaith organization. (4)

# 3.11

## Is it right to tell others about your faith?

In this topic you will consider the issues raised when people share their faith with others.

## Is it personal or not?

Many people get irritated if they are stopped in the street by someone who pushes a copy of a religious book or magazine at them, or questions them about God in public. But is religion such a personal matter that no one dare mention it in public? Isn't the twenty-first century a time when we can speak openly about things? Certainly, the Victorian taboo about mentioning sex in public has been dusted away; many people quite happily discuss contraception or issues of sexuality in public. What is so different about religion? Are we scared of the subject?

## The Christian attitude

Jesus taught his followers:

> *I am the way, the truth, and the life; no one goes to the Father except by me.*
> **(John 14:6)**

### Activity 1

a) What reasons might the man in the picture give for telling everyone about his religion?

b) What reasons might those who object give?

*Some Christians feel it is their religious duty to try to convert people to their religion. Why could this be a problem in a multi-faith society?*

Some Christians interpret this to mean that only people who follow Jesus' teachings will go to heaven, and so they feel they have a duty to try to put people on the right path by converting them to Christianity.

Liberal Christians are more likely to accept that Christianity is only one way to find God and different religions are another way that is equally valid. These Christians argue that Jesus never tried to convert Jews in his society, so they shouldn't either.

## The Muslim attitude

Muslims believe that everybody is born a Muslim, but some parents choose to bring their children up in another religion. The Qur'an teaches that people who accept Islam will go to heaven and those who do not will go to hell. This leads some Muslims to believe they have a duty to invite members of other faiths to learn about Islam and become Muslims. However, the Qur'an is very clear that nobody is to be forced to convert to Islam. Conversion is a matter for God and the person themselves, no one else.

## Something for sharing or keeping to yourself?

Members of both religions clearly feel that they have discovered something so wonderful it would be totally wrong not to share it with others. It is similar, perhaps, to a doctor discovering a cure for a devastating disease. They would feel it is their duty to share it with the rest of humanity, because anything else would be morally wrong.

Problems begin when others think that people preaching religion at them are invading their space. Equally, two or more religions claiming that they are the only ones to know the right way to God can also cause problems.

CHRIST DIED FOR THE UNGODLY

ROM. 5 v 6

# Religion and the media

*These TV evangelists lay their hands on Oral Roberts, a pioneer televangelist and faith healer.*

In the USA, it is common to find whole television stations given over to **evangelism**. Viewers of these sorts of programmes find that their faith is strengthened by watching them. Evangelical groups who run these television stations say they are using a modern way of spreading Jesus' message to reach people who wouldn't normally hear the Word of God. Opponents of Christian television channels see it as simply another form of 'hard sell' advertising, making religion little different from selling a car.

## Activity 2

For discussion: If someone discovers a vital piece of medical information that could improve people's lives, is it their duty to share it with everyone? Does this rule apply equally to religious information? Why?

## Check you have learnt:

- the meaning of 'evangelism'
- two reasons why some believers think evangelism is important
- two reasons why some people think evangelism is unacceptable.

## Activity 3

Try this (c) question:

> People should go out and spread the Word of God.

Give **two** reasons why a religious believer might agree or disagree with this statement. (4)

*The Salvation Army, who appeared on page 79, play hymns and carols in towns around Christmas. This is their way of spreading the Christian message to others. Do you think this sort of thing is harmful or should it be encouraged? Why?*

SHARING IS CARING

*Thank you!*

and

GOD BLESS YOU

THE SALVATION ARMY

NEED... KNOWS NO SEASON!

## TRY YOUR SKILL AT THIS

**The (e) question:**

'Evangelism is a good thing because if no one told you about a religion, you would never know about it.'

Do you agree? Give reasons or evidence for your answer, showing that you have thought of more than one point of view. You must include reference to religious beliefs in your answer. (8)

# SKILLS COACHING 9

## END OF CHAPTER 3 CHECK

### ✓ Check the (a) question

In this topic, we examined different ways that people express their faith. You have learnt these **KEY CONCEPTS**:

- community
- faith
- pilgrimage
- evangelism
- identity
- sacred

Choose three key concepts from the list and explain what they mean.

Which three key concepts did you not want to choose? Write down what you think their meanings might be and check them. Or, if you really don't know, then look them up in the topic and write down their meanings. It is better to face the difficult key concepts now!

What other important concepts have occurred in this topic that you could be asked?

### ✓ Check the (b) question

This is where you will be asked how having a religious faith affects someone's response to an issue. Remind yourself of the Christian and the Muslim responses to the issues below. Remember that you can choose to answer it from a general religious viewpoint with examples, but you may find it easier to concentrate on a particular religion you have studied:

- expressing faith through joining community worship
- expressing faith through going on pilgrimage
- expressing faith through religious symbols or clothing
- expressing faith through interfaith activities or evangelism.
- expressing faith through supporting a religious organization

### ✓ Check the (d) question

This question will be asking you to explain the response of two religious traditions to an issue. Make sure you know how Muslims and Christians respond and whether there are any differences within one religious tradition to the topics below:

- pilgrimage
- having a special place of worship
- wearing special clothes or symbols
- supporting a religious charity.

### ✓ Check the (c) and (e) questions

The (c) question is where you are offered a controversial statement in a speech bubble to comment on. In (c) questions the examiner is asking you to apply what you know about Christian or Muslim attitudes, or the attitudes of religious believers in general to the issues mentioned above. It is also quite acceptable to answer from two different standpoints within the same religion. For example in Christianity you might want to say '*The Catholic response is …*' with an example and explanation. Then you might follow it up by giving another Christian viewpoint from a Methodist perspective saying '*The Methodists think …*' and give an example with an explanation.

The (e) question is giving you a chance to have your say with supporting evidence. Rehearse the examples you would give and two or three pieces of evidence you could use to support your viewpoint. What would a religious believer say about this? Give an example and explanations. Revise the other side's views in the same way.

Here is a typical example of how a question on *Religious expression* might be presented on the exam paper. Try answering it in exam conditions in order to check your progress. Remember to use the visual stimuli. Look on page 37 to remind you how these can help.

(a) Explain what religious believers mean by 'evangelism'. (2)

(b) Explain how having a religious faith might encourage a person to work for a religious charity. (4)

> Religion is a private matter and not for sharing.

(c)

Give two reasons why a religious believer might agree or disagree with this statement. (4)

(i)                                        (ii)

(d) Explain from two different religious traditions how believers might express their faith through symbols in their place of worship. (You must state the religious traditions you are referring to.) (6)

(i)                                        (ii)

(e) 'Working for a charity is a better way of expressing faith than going on a pilgrimage.'

Do you agree? Give reasons or evidence for your answer, showing that you have thought of more than one point of view. You must include reference to religious beliefs in your answer. (8)

**In this topic you will look at human rights and why they are important.**

## What are human rights?

We are so used to people claiming 'It's my right' to do something or 'I've got my rights', but what do they really mean? And is it true? What **human rights** do people have? By human rights, we mean a person is entitled to certain freedoms because they are human beings.

## The Universal Declaration of Human Rights

After the human rights abuses of World War II, the United Nations (UN) drew up this declaration in 1948. The full text of it can be read on the UN's website (www.un.org/en/), but here are the main points:

1  Right to **equality**.
2  Freedom from discrimination.
3  Right to life, liberty and personal security.
4  Freedom from slavery.
5  Freedom from torture or degrading treatment.
6  Right to be recognized as a person by the law.
7  Right to equality before the law.
8  Right to a fair hearing if your rights are broken.
9  Freedom from arrest with no reason and exile.
10  Right to a fair public hearing if accused of something illegal.
11  Right to be considered innocent until proven guilty.
12  Freedom from interference with privacy, family, home and correspondence.
13  Right to free movement in and out of the country.
14  Right to asylum in other countries if being persecuted at home.
15  Right to a nationality and the freedom to change it.
16  Right to marriage and family.
17  Right to own property.
18  Freedom of belief and religion.
19  Freedom of opinion and information.
20  Right to meet peacefully with others and join groups.
21  Right to participate in government by voting and standing for election.
22  Right to social security.
23  Right to work safely for equal pay and to join a trade union.
24  Right to rest and leisure.
25  Right to an adequate living standard.
26  Right to an education.
27  Right to participate in cultural activity, e.g. the arts.
28  Right to have society run in a way which protects your rights.
29  Everyone has duties but these should only help achieve everyone's rights in society, they cannot harm rights.
30  Everyone should be free from interference in their rights.

### KEY CONCEPTS KEY C

**human rights** something a person is entitled to because they are human

**justice** where everyone has equal provisions and opportunity

*Useful specialist language*

**equality** the belief that everyone should have the same rights

### Activity 1

With a partner, list **ten** things you both agree a person is entitled to simply because they are human.

Although the UK has a long history of concern for the abuse of human rights, the Human Rights Act has only had a place in British law since 1998.

## Why should religious people be concerned about human rights?

The answer lies in the word 'human' because members of most religions believe humans were created by God. It follows then that God's creation must be treated with respect. On pages 40–41 you learnt about the sanctity of life idea, and that too has a place in human rights. If life is sacred, it must mean that people have special rights that must be protected. Most religions agree on this and it is summed up by the idea that you should treat others as you would like to be treated yourself. As you will discover on pages 118–119 and 122–123 in this chapter, religious believers look to their scriptures for authority on how to put human rights into practice.

## It's only fair

Even those with no particular religious faith still believe humans have rights that should be preserved. Helping the weaker members of our society is regarded by many simply as **justice**. It's only right, they say, that everybody should have the same opportunities and access to things as everyone else. By helping those who can't look after themselves in our society, it raises us above the level of other animals.

### Activity 2

Explain why human rights are totally different to the laws of the animal kingdom.

**Check you have learnt:**

- what is meant by 'human rights'
- two reasons why religious believers support human rights
- why justice must involve human rights.

### Activity 3

Try this (c) question:

> Everybody has to fight for their rights; that is part of life.

Give **two** reasons why a religious believer might agree or disagree with this statement. (4)

**TRY YOUR SKILL AT THIS**

**The (e) question:**

'It's impossible to give everybody equal rights, we are all different.'

Do you agree? Give reasons or evidence for your answer, showing that you have thought of more than one point of view. You must include reference to religious beliefs in your answer. (8)

# 4.2

## Why do Christians and Muslims believe human rights are important?

In this topic you will examine the reasons why human rights are important to Christians and Muslims.

## Activity 1

What does the following biblical passage teach a Christian about human rights?

> *From one human being he created all races on earth and made them live throughout the whole earth.*
> **(Act 17:26)**

## Christians believe in human rights

There are many biblical passages that teach Christians the importance of human rights. In the very first book of the Bible, Genesis, it says:

> *Adam named his wife Eve, because she was the mother of all human beings.*
> **(Genesis 3:20)**

This shows we are all related. Modern science uses DNA to prove this is true. If everybody is related, then it means they are all entitled to the same rights – human rights.

## The example of Jesus

What Jesus said and how he behaved also teaches Christians how important human rights are. The Gospels tell of times when Jesus went out of his way to ensure people who had been rejected by everyone else still received fair treatment. There are accounts of Jesus healing a leper whom nobody would go near, of dealing kindly with a prostitute and a tax collector as well as responding to a request for help from a Roman soldier. All of these people would have been disliked by Jewish society and ignored whenever possible.

The Catholic Church believes human rights matter:

> *[E]ach individual man is truly a person. His is a nature, that is, endowed with intelligence and free will. As such he has rights and duties … . These rights and duties are universal and inviolable.*
> **(Pope John XXIII)**

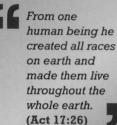

*Some Christians and Muslims put their concern about human rights into practice by buying goods that they know have been fairly traded, like these bananas. Religious believers are concerned that many products we buy cheaply in the UK have actually been produced by workers who are paid very low wages and are forced to work in appalling conditions. This is an abuse of their human rights, which the Bible teaches Christians is wrong and the Qur'an teaches Muslims is wrong.*

*One of the 99 names of Allah is Al-Hakam, which means 'The Judge'. This shows Muslims how important it is to treat people justly because Allah will judge them accordingly on the Day of Judgement.*

## Muslims believe in human rights

The Qur'an teaches Muslims that everyone was created by Allah and Allah treats everyone equally. This means that Allah expects everyone to treat each other in the same way. Those who do not treat others equally will be judged accordingly when they go before Allah on the Day of Judgement. If they have discriminated against people, they cannot expect Allah to show mercy to them. On the Day of Judgement, the good will be rewarded and the evil punished.

## The example of Muhammad

Religious believers look to the teachings and the example of Muhammad for guidance about equal rights. Muhammad treated everyone fairly no matter what their race and he chose Bilal, a black African Muslim, to call people to prayer. In his last sermon, Muhammad reminded his followers:

> *All mankind is from Adam and Eve, an Arab has not superiority over a non-Arab, nor a non-Arab has any superiority over black, nor black has any superiority over white except by piety and good action.*

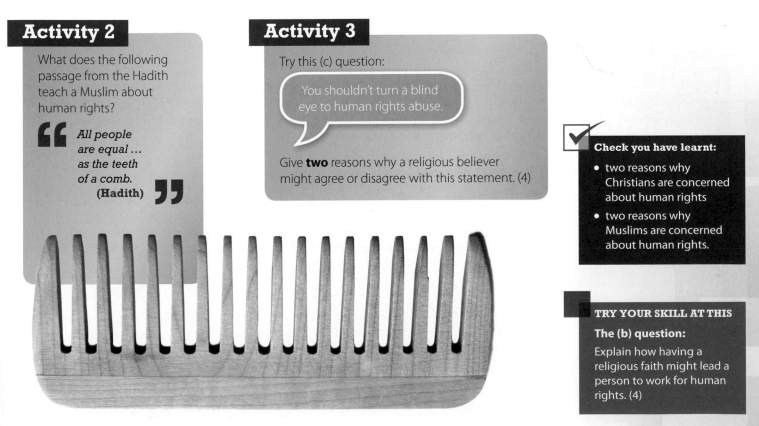

### Activity 2

What does the following passage from the Hadith teach a Muslim about human rights?

> *All people are equal … as the teeth of a comb.* **(Hadith)**

### Activity 3

Try this (c) question:

> You shouldn't turn a blind eye to human rights abuse.

Give **two** reasons why a religious believer might agree or disagree with this statement. (4)

**Check you have learnt:**

- two reasons why Christians are concerned about human rights
- two reasons why Muslims are concerned about human rights.

**TRY YOUR SKILL AT THIS**

**The (b) question:**

Explain how having a religious faith might lead a person to work for human rights. (4)

# Oscar Romero

**In this topic you will learn about a religious believer who has worked for human rights.**

Oscar Romero became a priest at the age of 25 and settled down to work in his parish in San Salvador, the South American country where he was born. For over 20 years, Romero quietly cared for his parishioners and in 1970 was appointed an auxiliary bishop. Seven years later, he became Archbishop of San Salvador. The government was not concerned about this appointment because Romero had never involved himself in politics in the past.

## A murder changed everything

Within a fortnight of Archbishop Romero's appointment, his life changed dramatically. His friend, the priest Rutilio Grande, was executed by a government death squad for trying to organize the poor into a trade union to stop them being exploited by their wealthy employers.

*Oscar Romero (1917–80).*

> *When I looked at Rutilio lying there dead, I thought: if they killed him for doing what he did, then I too have to walk the same path.* **(Oscar Romero)**

### Activity 1

Try this (c) question:

> It's madness to speak out when you know you will be killed.

Give **two** reasons why a religious believer might agree or disagree with this statement. (4)

Life was never the same for Romero again. He demanded that the government investigate Rutilio's killing, but nothing happened. The newspapers could never report anything because they were censored by the government. All around him Romero saw terrible things happening. Death squads roamed the countryside picking on anyone who dared to protest. Men, women and children were beaten up or simply 'vanished'.

## The need to speak out

Romero could not keep silent when he saw rich landowners making huge profits whilst their employees starved to death. Those like Rutilio who tried to help the poor were severely punished. As the country's archbishop, Oscar Romero had a **personal conviction** that he must use his power and influence to tell the world what was going on in San Salvador, even if he risked his own life.

### Activity 2

Write a paragraph explaining what abuses in San Salvador horrified Oscar Romero.

> *We suffer with those who have disappeared, those who have had to flee their homes and those who have been tortured.* **(Oscar Romero)**

In his radio broadcasts, Romero condemned the government for human rights abuses and its reign of terror where torture and assassinations were commonplace.

# Inspired by Jesus

People were shocked at how outspoken Romero became, but he said he was simply trying to follow in Jesus' footsteps. Jesus never sat back and let evil flourish; he stood up for what he knew to be right even though it cost him his life. Romero knew the price he was likely to pay for drawing everyone's attention to the plight of the poor in his country.

> *If they kill me, I shall arise again in the Salvadoran people. Let my blood be a seed of freedom, and the sign that hope will soon be a reality.* **(Oscar Romero)**

People around the world heard Romero's broadcasts and some took notice. The government retaliated by bombing his radio station twice. But the Christian charity CAFOD (see pages 72–73) came to Romero's aid by paying to rebuild it.

# On the international stage

For three years, Romero took every opportunity to tell the world how the poor suffered. In February 1980, he made a public appeal to the president of the USA, Jimmy Carter, to stop supplying weapons to San Salvador because these weapons were being used to repress the ordinary people.

The San Salvador government was furious and stepped up efforts to silence Romero. He received death threats, but ignored them. Even the murder of six priests on government orders could not silence Romero.

> *If God accepts the sacrifice of my life, may my death be for the freedom of my people … A bishop will die, but the Church of God, which is the people, will never perish.* **(Oscar Romero)**

A bomb was found behind the pulpit in Romero's church, but it failed to explode. In what proved to be his final sermon, Romero appealed to the soldiers in his country to stop the massacres:

> *Brothers, you came from our own people. You are killing your own brother peasants when any human order to kill must be subordinate to the law of God, which says, 'Thou shalt not kill'. No soldier is obliged to obey an order contrary to the law of God. No one has to obey an immoral law. It is high time you recovered your consciences and obeyed your consciences rather than a sinful order. The church cannot remain silent before such an abomination. In the name of God, in the name of this suffering people whose cries rise to heaven more loudly each day, I implore you, I beg you, I order you – in the name of God: stop the repression.* **(Oscar Romero)**

The following day, as Romero was celebrating mass in the chapel at a cancer hospital, a bullet was fired through an open window and killed him. Romero's last words were: "May God have mercy on the assassin."

## Activity 3

Explain how Archbishop Romero's actions were motivated by Jesus.

## Check you have learnt:

- the name of one religious believer who worked for human rights
- what he did for human rights
- how his religion inspired him.

## TRY YOUR SKILL AT THIS

**The (e) question:**

'A religious person should be prepared to sacrifice their life for human rights.'

Do you agree? Give reasons for your answer, showing you have thought of more than one point of view. You must include reference to religious beliefs in your answer. (8)

# SKILLS COACHING 10

## DO YOU UNDERSTAND?

### Improve your skill with the (a) question

Write the meaning of these **KEY CONCEPTS** words from memory:

- justice
- human rights
- personal conviction

### Improve your skill with the (b) question

Here you link the way a person behaves, or their attitude to an issue, to their religious beliefs. Your answer has to contain specialist language or a key concept. Try answering the following (b) question:

> Explain how having a religious faith might support the view that human rights matter.  (4)

Remember: **POINT + EXAMPLE + EXPLANATION**

Tackle this question step by step.

> ❋ **TRY THIS** ❋
> Work with a partner and each select four key concepts and meanings from earlier topics in this textbook. Make them difficult! In fact, choose the four that you found hardest to remember because, by doing so, it will help you to fix their meanings in your mind. Now challenge your partner to give you the correct definition. Swap round and see who wins. You can play it as a class game if you prefer.

**STEP 1** Underline the **important words** in the question.

**STEP 2** Look at **the stimulus** to see if there is anything that might help you there.

**STEP 3** Decide **what religion, or religions**, you want to use and what their teachings are. Don't forget you are free to write from a general religious viewpoint if you feel confident that you have got good evidence.

**STEP 4** Decide what **key concept** or **specialist language** you will be using. Finally, write up your answer in full sentences.

### Improve your skill with the (d) question

It is worth making a big effort to revise the different responses Muslims and Christians have to the issues you have studied and to any differences within the one religion. In your work so far on this topic, *Authority – religion and state*, you will need to revise:

- why Muslims believe human rights matter
- why Christians believe human rights matter.

HINT

When a (d) question asks you to *Explain from two different religious traditions* about something, it is possible to choose to answer from two different Christian traditions. There are issues you have studied where there is a distinct difference of opinion about an issue within the different branches of Christianity. If you are sure of your facts and can name the two branches of Christianity and their teachings, you can answer exclusively from Christianity.

# WHAT DO PEOPLE THINK?

## Improve your skill with the (c) question

Based on what you have studied in Chapter 4, **Authority – religion and state**, you can predict that any statements on the material so far will be concerned with whether or not human rights are important; whether equal rights for everyone is realistic and the role of justice within human rights.

Create two controversial statements about this subject matter and share them with the group. This can be a very helpful way of thinking about this material from a different angle. It also helps you to realize there are only so many ways a question on this can be phrased and, as a group, you have probably spotted most of them!

Now is a good time in your studies to remind yourself of the step-by-step approach to tackling the (c) question, that cheerful little speech bubble that turns up with some awkward statements.

Choose one of the controversial statements made up by your group and judged to be a good one. Write it in a speech bubble and add the rest of the wording for part (c) of Question 4:

Give two reasons why a religious believer might agree or disagree with this statement.

Now use the step-by-step method to write a high level answer to a (c) question.

### STEP 1

Underline the important words in the statement.

### STEP 2

Choose which religion, religions, or general religious viewpoints you are going to use in your answer. Write that down.

### STEP 3

What are the religious teachings on this subject? Note them down. Does it look like the religion will be totally in agreement or disagreement? Or might there be different interpretations on this issue?

### STEP 4

Choose two religious examples to use in your answer. Choose the ones that you can explain the best.

Finally, write up your answer. You could begin. *'The ... religion would agree/disagree with this statement for two reasons ...'* then give your example and explanation for each one as fully as you can.

## Improve your skill with the (e) question

Remember the (e) part of each question carries the most marks. That is because it is testing several things.

1 The examiner wants you to show that you can apply the religious teachings that you learnt to a modern-day topic by explaining why a believer will take a certain view on it with an example and explanations.

2 At the same time you are being asked to give your own opinion of this subject with a **point + an example + evidence or explanations**.

3 The examiner is also interested in your use of English in this question. What they are looking at particularly is the way you communicate the information, the overall readability of your answer.

So, no pressure there then!

Try your ever-improving skills on this (e) question:

'Equal rights for all is impossible.'

Do you agree? Give reasons or evidence for your answer, showing that you have thought of more than one point of view. You must include reference to religious beliefs in your answer. (8)

# What is the point of punishment?

**In this topic you will study the aims and purpose of punishment.**

**KEY CONCEPTS**

**punishment** a penalty given to someone for a crime or wrong they have done

Laws only work if crime is seen to be punished. Here are some of the theories regarding the aims of **punishment**. Most punishments contain a mixture of these things. One thing everyone agrees on is that the punishment should make criminals take responsibility for their actions.

## 1. Protection

Punishing a wrongdoer by locking them in prison, or taking their life, in order to protect society from the criminal. Does this work as well for a debtor as for a child abuser?

## 2. Deterrent

Having a sufficiently harsh punishment to discourage others from breaking the law. A deterrent is also likely to discourage a criminal from re-offending, or someone else from committing a similar crime. Would this work for 'crimes of passion' where a husband comes in and finds his wife in bed with another man, then attacks that man?

## 3. Retribution

Punishing a person in order to make them pay for what they have done. Retribution is sometimes summed up as 'an eye for an eye'. Does this punishment work for a person who assists someone with voluntary euthanasia?

## 4. Reform

A method of punishment that aims to stop a criminal from re-offending. Reform can be achieved through a programme of education and training in prison. Will society be content for the unemployed murderer to be enrolled on a course for plumbers?

## Activity 1

Create a table or spreadsheet and list each of the six punishment theories. Note down the advantages and disadvantages of each punishment.

## 5. Reparation

Through punishment, a criminal is made to pay for their crime by doing something to help society or the victim. Once a criminal has settled this debt, they are rehabilitated into society and can start life afresh. Is it sufficient for the drink-driver to pay a large fine to the family of the deceased?

## 6. Vindication

If a society has laws, then it must have a system of punishment in place to show its laws are of supreme importance and must be kept.

## Activity 2

Which of the theories of punishment can be applied to putting criminals in jail? Do you think prisons are an effective form of punishment?

## Activity 3

Try this (c) question:

> Depriving someone of their freedom is the best punishment for murder.

Give **two** reasons why a religious believer might agree or disagree with this statement. (4)

## Activity 4

### YOB SMASHES PENSIONER'S GREENHOUSE

In court today, Mark Pratt, 14, said he was 'messing about' near the allotments but admitted he was drunk and couldn't remember anything. Eyewitnesses saw him throwing stones at the greenhouse.

### YOUNG WOMAN SHOPLIFTER SENTENCED

Paula Simpson, 17, was arrested as she walked out of 'Nightshades' with two designer handbags, worth £265, which she had not paid for. She asked for seven other offences to be taken into consideration.

a) With a partner, choose **one** of the newspaper stories. Taking each of the theories of punishment in turn, decide:
- what punishment should be given for the offence
- whether the punishment would work
- if the punishment is just.

b) As a class, discuss which punishment most people feel would be appropriate for each offence and why.

**Check you have learnt:**
- how punishments can serve different purposes
- four different theories of punishment
- the strengths and weaknesses of punishments.

**TRY YOUR SKILL AT THIS**

**The (e) question:**

'Trying to reform criminals is a waste of time.'

Do you agree? Give reasons for your answer, showing you have thought of more than one point of view. You must include reference to religious beliefs in your answer. (8)

**In this topic you will examine the arguments for and against capital punishment.**

### Useful specialist language

**capital punishment** the death penalty for a crime or offence

*In 2000, Dr Harold Shipman was convicted of killing 15 patients. An enquiry concluded the number could be closer to 250. Shipman was sentenced to prison for the rest of his life, but committed suicide in 2004.*

## Activity 1

a) What arguments could be put forward to support the death penalty for Harold Shipman, the UK's worst serial killer? Give your reasons.

b) Would you have supported the death penalty for Harold Shipman? Give your reasons.

## What is capital punishment?

*Capital punishment* means using execution as the punishment for a crime or offence. Only the State or a recognized authority can do this after they have held a proper trial. Anyone else who executes a person is committing murder.

Capital punishment is still used legally in 71 countries around the world, but the UN is working towards its abolition. In the UK, the last person to be executed was in 1964; the death penalty was finally abolished for all crimes in the UK in 1998. However, the reintroduction of the death penalty is regularly discussed for crimes such as murdering a policeman.

## A few facts about the death penalty:

A total of 2390 people were put to death in 2008, up from 1252 in 2007. A further 8864 people were sentenced to death in 2008.

Amnesty's figures show that China executed 1718 people in 2008, which is 72% of the total number of people put to death in the year. This figure represents a minimum estimate – the real figure is undoubtedly higher.

Iran has the second-highest figure for executions; in 2008 they recorded 346 deaths, including eight juveniles.

The six countries with the highest execution figures are China (at least 1718), Iran (at least 346), Saudi Arabia (at least 102), USA (37), Pakistan (at least 36) and Iraq (at least 34).

Thirty-six American states have the death penalty. Nine of these states carried out executions in 2008, and just under half of the executions that took place in America in 2008 were carried out in Texas.

The only country in Europe that still executes prisoners is Belarus.

# Those in favour of capital punishment say:

- It is an excellent deterrent. Knowing that they could be executed for a crime is likely to stop most people committing it in the first place.
- The death penalty removes dangerous people, like terrorists and serial killers, from society, making it a safer place for us all. It certainly stops re-offending.
- The death penalty is far cheaper than keeping a criminal in a maximum security prison for the rest of their life at the State's expense.
- A life for a life is fair retribution. Human life is the most valuable thing a person has, so a murderer should lose theirs.
- The death penalty gives the victim's family a sense of closure, which helps them to get on with their lives.

# Those against capital punishment say:

- Innocent people get convicted by mistake; using the death penalty prevents mistakes being corrected.
- Life is sacred; no one has the right to kill another person.
- Life in prison is a greater deterrent to many criminals, which is why some try to commit suicide.
- If there is a death penalty for murder, there is nothing to stop a person killing many people.
- The death penalty is inhuman and barbaric; it creates a brutal society.
- A UN survey in 1988 and 1996 found no evidence that capital punishment was a deterrent.
- Terrorists who are executed are sometimes regarded as heroes or martyrs, which might encourage others to follow.

Amnesty International opposes the death penalty in all cases without exception, regardless of the nature of the crime, who the offender is or the method used to kill. They believe that the death penalty violates a fundamental

human right – the right to life – as laid down in the Universal Declaration of Human Rights. Amnesty International believe that the death penalty is an ultimately cruel, inhuman and degrading punishment, and has not been shown to have a deterrent effect on others.

## Activity 2

a) Look back to the theories of punishment on page 108. Read through each one and decide whether capital punishment fits the criteria. Share your conclusions with the class.

b) Take a class vote on whether the death penalty should be reinstated in the UK.

## Activity 3

Try this (c) question:

> Capital punishment is a form of murder.

Give **two** reasons why a religious believer might agree or disagree with this statement. (4)

✓ **Check you have learnt:**

- what capital punishment means
- four reasons to support capital punishment
- four reasons to oppose capital punishment.

**TRY YOUR SKILL AT THIS**

**The (e) question:**

'A life for a life is fair.'

Do you agree? Give reasons or evidence for your answer, showing that you have thought of more than one point of view. You must include reference to religious beliefs in your answer. (8)

## CASE STUDY

In London in 1953, Derek Bentley, aged 19, was hanged for the murder of a policeman in a robbery that went wrong. The shot that killed the policeman was fired by Chris Craig, his accomplice, who was aged 16. Both were found guilty of murder, but Craig went to prison because he was underage. Bentley was sentenced to death because he was alleged to have told Craig to 'Let him have it, Chris'. Bentley had learning difficulties and a mental age of 11. In 1998, the Court of Appeal overturned Bentley's conviction for murder. Craig served ten years in prison and has remained out of trouble ever since.

## Activity 4

a) Why was the case of Derek Bentley controversial?

b) What does it add to the debate about capital punishment?

## Why is justice important to Christians?

**In this topic you will look at Christian beliefs about justice, punishment and the death penalty.**

The Bible teaches Christians that God is just and expects his people to treat each other in the same way. Treating people unjustly is a sin and those who do so can expect to pay the penalty on the Day of Judgement.

The Old Testament idea of justice was retribution. It said, '… the punishment shall be life for life, eye for eye, tooth for tooth' and continued on to a 'bruise for bruise' (Exodus 21:23–5). However, it also made clear that once punishment was given, that was the end. Vendettas and long-running disputes were unjust.

### Activity 1

Jesus' message is often referred to as 'turning the other cheek'. Read the quotation from Matthew 5:38–9 and explain what this means. Could it work? Why?

## Jesus' teachings about justice

Jesus' teachings about justice were revolutionary because he linked justice with non-violence and forgiveness. He taught that retribution was wrong and it was better to use love to overcome injustice. Forgiving a person who has hurt you, Jesus said, was better than exacting punishment.

> *You have heard that it was said, 'An eye for an eye, and a tooth for a tooth.' But now I tell you: do not take revenge on someone who wrongs you. If anyone slaps you on the right cheek, let him slap your left cheek too.* **(Matthew 5:38–9)**

## Fighting injustice

Jesus taught people to share their wealth with those who have none to create a fairer and just society. This has led Christians to give money to charity and to take part in projects to share the earth's resources more fairly. Christians also believe that there is an unjust division of wealth in the world, which leads them to campaign against poverty in less economically developed countries. 'Make Poverty History' and 'Drop the Debt' are campaigns that Christians actively support. Buying goods that have been fairly traded is another way Christians fight injustice.

## Capital punishment

Whilst all Christians agree that human life is sacred and killing is wrong, some make an exception when it comes to taking a life in war or as punishment for crime.

*This is death row in the state of California in America. Some Christians who are against capital punishment visit the inmates to bring them comfort. Other Christians believe that human life is sacred, so it is just for a murderer to pay for their crime with their own life.*

## The Bible leads some Christians to support capital punishment

The Old Testament has many teachings about the death penalty which Christians, who accept the Bible as the Word of God, use to justify their belief in capital punishment:

> If anyone takes human life, he will be punished … Human beings were made like God, so whoever murders one of them will himself be killed by someone else. **(Genesis 9:5–6)**

In the New Testament, St Paul told Christians:

> Everyone must obey the state authorities, because no authority exists without God's permission, and the existing authorities have been put there by God. **(Romans 13:1)**

This means that if capital punishment is part of a country's legal code, Christians must accept that law. Jesus also taught his followers to obey the law of the land. In the past, the Christian Church used the death penalty as a punishment for heresy.

Christians who support the death penalty would also use non-religious reasons like those on page 111 to support their case.

## The reasons why some Christians are against capital punishment

- Jesus brought a message of love and compassion. He emphasized the importance of forgiveness not retribution.

- Jesus said he had come to save sinners. However, if the state executes a criminal, there is no chance for Christians to save them from their sins or help them to reform their behaviour.

- The Bible teaches Christians that only God can give life and only God can take it away. This does not permit anyone, or any authority, to execute a person. If Christians use these teachings to forbid abortion and euthanasia, some argue they must also apply them to the death penalty.

- Old Testament punishments belonged to an ancient society. Today's society has different attitudes and other ways of dealing with offenders.

- For some Christians, the sixth commandment 'Do not commit murder' means that no one is permitted to kill anybody.

- There is evidence that some people who have suffered the death penalty in the past were mentally ill, or trapped in a life of crime and poverty because they had little choice. Jesus came to save people like this and Christians believe it is their duty to do the same.

**Activity 2**

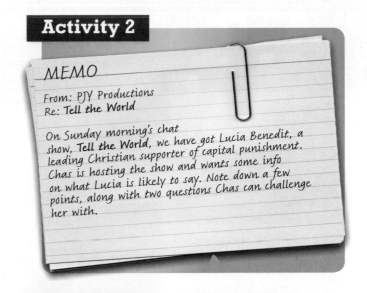

MEMO

From: PJY Productions
Re: Tell the World

On Sunday morning's chat show, Tell the World, we have got Lucia Benedit, a leading Christian supporter of capital punishment. Chas is hosting the show and wants some info on what Lucia is likely to say. Note down a few points, along with two questions Chas can challenge her with.

*Because Jesus suffered the death penalty for a crime he did not commit, some Christians hold strong views against capital punishment.*

**Activity 3**

Using a spreadsheet or table, record the arguments Christians might use for and against capital punishment. Don't forget to include the non-religious points on page 111.

**Check you have learnt:**

- what justice means to Christians
- two different Christian attitudes to the death penalty
- what Jesus taught Christians about justice.

**TRY YOUR SKILL AT THIS**

**The (b) question:**

Explain how having a religious faith might influence a person's attitude to punishment. (4)

**Activity 4**

Try this (c) question:

No Christian should agree with the death penalty.

Give **two** reasons why a religious believer might agree or disagree with this statement. (4)

In this topic you will look at Muslim beliefs about justice, punishment and the death penalty.

*One of the 99 names of Allah is Al-Hakam, which means 'The Just'. This teaches Muslims how important justice is.*

## Allah is just

Justice is extremely important to Muslims because they believe that Allah is just. He created everybody equal and treats his creation with justice and fairness. Allah expects everybody to treat each other in the same way.

Those who do not treat other people with justice will be judged accordingly when they go before Allah on the Day of Judgement. If they have not shown mercy to others, they cannot expect Allah to show mercy to them. On the Day of Judgement, the good will be rewarded and the evil punished; that is the justice of Allah.

Muslims believe they have a **duty** to work towards a just society and the Qur'an gives them guidance.

> *Those who seek to redress their wrongs incur no guilt. But great is the guilt of those who oppress their fellow men and conduct themselves with wickedness and injustice in the land. Woeful punishment awaits them.* **(Qur'an 42:40)**

### Activity 1

Rephrase the quotation from the Qur'an in your own words. What does it teach Muslims about justice?

### Useful specialist language

**Shari'ah law** a code of law based on the teachings of the Qur'an and the practice of the prophet Muhammad

## Shari'ah law

Muslims are taught that it is Allah's will that they should follow the straight path of life set out in the Qur'an. The Islamic legal system is called **Shari'ah law**. It is based on the idea of justice for everyone and it puts the teachings of the Qur'an into laws. All Muslims are entitled to equal treatment under Shari'ah law. Islamic courts use Shari'ah law to decide on just punishments if the laws of Allah are broken.

## Justice is most important

Islam is a religion that is based on peace and justice. For some crimes, Muslims believe that death is a just punishment. To let someone off would be an injustice for the victim and their family, it would also be damaging to society. Although society must punish a criminal for their behaviour, Muslims believe that Allah will be the ultimate judge and he will punish them in the afterlife.

Islam regards the death penalty as the correct form of retribution for some crimes. Capital punishment is also regarded as a deterrent and a punishment that safeguards people's lives and property.

Capital punishment can only be legal if the accused is given a fair trial in a court of law and found guilty. Other less severe punishments are also possible under Shari'ah law and these must be weighed up against the crime. However, in the most severe cases, capital punishment is believed to be the just punishment.

### Activity 2

Try this (c) question:

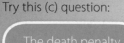 The death penalty is a just punishment for murder.

Give **two** reasons why a religious believer might agree or disagree with this statement. (4)

*Islam permits the death penalty to be carried out by firing squad, beheading, hanging or stoning.*

> *… whoever killed a human being, except as punishment for murder or other villainy in the land, shall be regarded as having killed all mankind; and that whoever saved a human life shall be regarded as having saved all mankind.*
> **(Qur'an 5:32)**

> *… you shall not kill – for that is forbidden by God – except for a just cause.* **(Qur'an 6:151)**

Shari'ah law permits the death penalty for:

- **deliberate murder**. The family of a victim has the right to say whether or not they wish the murderer to be executed.
- **threatening to undermine the authority**. This is a wide area, which is interpreted in different ways that range from treason and terrorism to adultery and homosexuality. It also permits the death penalty for a Muslim who rejects their religion and actively works against it.

## Not all Muslims demand the death penalty

Some Muslims point out that the Qur'an does permit other punishments. For instance, the family of a victim is permitted to pardon the criminal and accept a payment of 'blood money' rather than insist on execution. Whilst all Muslim countries have the death penalty on their statute books, some countries have not used it for many years.

### Activity 3

For discussion: Is it a good idea to let a victim's family decide on the right punishment? Why? Note down the points given for and against this.

**Check you have learnt:**

- why justice is important to Muslims
- why most Muslims accept the need for capital punishment
- why some Muslims do not agree with capital punishment.

### TRY YOUR SKILL AT THIS

**The (d) question:**

Explain from **two** different traditions the teachings about capital punishment. (You must state the religious traditions you are referring to.) (6)

**Hint**: Use these pages along with pages 110–111 to answer from the Christian and Muslim traditions.

### Improve your skill with the (a) question

Can you identify the correct **KEY CONCEPTS** to match the definitions?

? = something a person is entitled to because they are human.

? = where everyone has equal provision and opportunity.

? = a penalty given to someone for a crime or wrong they have done.

? = something a person strongly feels or believes in.

? = something you do because it is the accepted pattern of behaviour.

> **Tip**
> Don't forget that justice is an issue for the victims of crime, as well as the people who commit those crimes.

### Improve your skill with the (b) question

Here you are asked to link someone's religious beliefs with their behaviour. Since the whole of this chapter is on **Authority – religion and state** many of the questions will be about the way we treat people who break the rules in our society. You could revise the way people treat each other in terms of their human rights. At the same time, think about how these teachings can be put into practice in terms of treating people who break the law and those who are victims of crime, or whether it is ever right to take the life of a killer.

### Improve your skill with the (d) question

This is the 6 mark question and well worth spending extra time revising. The topics you will need to study for the complete topic **Authority – religion and state** are:

- Christian and Muslim attitudes to human rights
- Christian and Muslim teachings about justice
- Christian and Muslim teachings about duty to others
- Christian and Muslim attitudes towards capital punishment.

Remember: There may be different attitudes towards each of the topics above within the one religion.

Choose one from this list. Put a line down the centre of your page and head one column '*Christian*' and the other column '*Muslim*'. Then jot down from memory the relevant teachings. (Don't forget to include different attitudes within the one religion.)

Circle the teachings that are shared. Be aware of their differences. Fill in some specialist language. Any key concepts to go in?

Now go ahead and answer the question that begins:

> Explain from two different religious traditions the teachings about …. (fill in the subject you have chosen.)

Aim for 6 marks!

Neil aimed for 6 marks in his answer to the question about human rights teachings. Read it and decide whether you think he achieved his goal. Give Neil a mark for his answer and some comments. If you think it did not achieve the highest level please tell him what he needs to do to get those 6 marks.

> *Muslims believe that Allah wants us to treat everybody equally because the Qur'an says they must. They think Allah will judge them badly if they are unjust to another human being. On the Day of Judgement, Muslims could go to hell for abusing anyone's human rights. Muslims also believe Allah treats all the people he created equally, no matter what race or gender they are so they have got to do the same. Christians agree with this.*

Look on page 128 to see what the examiner had to say about Neil's answer.

# WHAT DO PEOPLE THINK?

## Improve your skill with the (e) question

At the same time as making a final push to get the 6 marks offered for a (d) question, it is worth making an extra effort with the other high-mark question on the paper: the (e) question.

The material that you just studied in this topic on **Authority – religion and state** has been concerned with justice and equal rights and with how members of a faith deal with the issue of punishment.

AIM HIGH

The question is asking you to:

> Give reasons or evidence for your answer, showing that you have thought of more than one point of view.

And it goes on to remind you to refer to religious beliefs in your answer. One way to really impress the examiner is to refer to **two** different religious traditions in your answer. Now that is smart! It shows that you have a really good grasp of the different ways religions respond to things. Alternatively you might be able to refer to the way one religion actually has two different responses to an issue.

If both religions have the same response to an issue, don't say 'they think the same' – you won't get any marks. You need to spell out clearly what each religion thinks and why, for example *'Christians believe in defending human rights because... . Muslims also believe in defending human rights because... .'*

Being able to support your point with a well-developed explanation or plenty of evidence also impresses the examiner. In fact the more evidence you give, the more there is for the examiner to reward.

Planning your (e) answer:

**1** Begin by looking at the statement. Make sure you are clear what it is saying. Underline any significant words so you keep focused.

**2** Then decide what you think about it. Do you agree? Or do you disagree?

**3** Because nobody's opinion is worth much without being backed up, decide what example you are going to use. Ideally you should try to offer two pieces of evidence or explanation but it may be that you have one very good reason that you want to explain fully. Great! That is just as valid.

**4** *'On the other hand ...'* is an excellent way to start the second paragraph. That's because it will lead you into telling the examiner what people who disagree with you say. Once again you should be looking for a **point + example + two good reasons or one well-developed explanation**.

**5** *'So I think ...'* is a good way to round off your answer with a final third paragraph. Only one sentence is necessary for the conclusion where you are re-stating your response to the quotation briefly.

**6** When it's written, check the English in this (e) question particularly closely. Have you written in sentences? Have you used capital letters and full stops? Have you divided your different points of view into paragraphs? Have you used some specialist language? And cast an eye over those spellings.

Here is an (e) question for you to practise:

> 'If God is the judge we have no right to punish people.'
>
> Do you agree? Give reasons or evidence for your answer, showing that you have thought of more than one point of view. You must include reference to religious beliefs in your answer. (8)

**In this topic you will examine the way some Christians use the Bible as a basis for making moral decisions.**

## KEY CONCEPTS KEY

**authority** right or power over others

### Useful specialist language

**conscience** an inner feeling of the rightness or wrongness of action

**moral decisions** these are answers to difficult personal questions about right and wrong behaviour, for example in matters such as relationships or honesty

**revelation** the belief that the scriptures were directly inspired by God and can reveal the truth to those who read them

## Activity 1

Try this (c) question:

> There is nothing special about a book of rules, your conscience is better.

Give **two** reasons why a religious believer might agree or disagree with this statement. (4)

## How do Christians know what is right and what is wrong?

It is easy for people to say, 'You should do the right thing,' but how does anybody know what's right and what's wrong? What is needed is a source of **authority** that is easily accessible and totally reliable.

Christians look to God as the ultimate source of authority to decide what is right and what is wrong. This might seem straightforward enough, except, Christians look in different places to consult God's authority. This diagram shows some of those places.

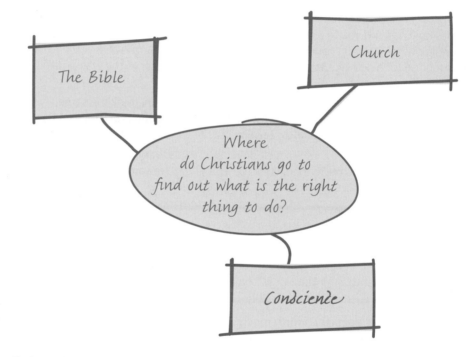

The Bible

Church

Where do Christians go to find out what is the right thing to do?

Condcienze

### Look in a book

For hundreds of years, books have been accepted as the best source of authority. People trust what they see in print, believing it has stood the test of time. Today, the computer has largely taken its place as a method of checking facts. Where would you automatically look if you had to find out the date of the first printed copy of the Bible? Whilst it is likely you would use the Internet, you'd probably be looking at the written word on screen – an electronic book in effect.

For some Christians, the Bible is the best source of authority.

HOLY BIBLE

## What makes the Bible special?

Christians believe that the Bible is no ordinary book because it was inspired by God. This means that what is written there has God's authority. The Bible, which has been in existence for hundreds of years, contains rules and teachings telling people how to lead their lives. These are the parts some Christians turn to when they need answers to difficult moral questions.

- **The rules** – Christians are most likely to consult the Ten Commandments, which they regard as God-given rules. They are found in the Old Testament part of the Bible. Also found there are many other rules about the way people should behave.

- **The teachings** – for Christians, the most important teachings are those given by Jesus, the Son of God, and these are found in the New Testament. Jesus' Sermon on the Mount tells followers about the sort of lives God wants people to lead. Jesus told many parables, or stories, to help people understand his teachings better. Christians also read the teachings of St Paul, who lived after Jesus and wrote a large number of letters to assist newly-formed Christian groups to make the right *moral decisions*.

- **Revelation** – some Christians believe that if they read and meditate on their holy scriptures, the truth of God's message will be revealed directly to them.

## Different attitudes towards the authority of the Bible

- For some Christians, the Bible contains the words of God, quite literally. This means that the Bible must be consulted and followed as closely as possible.

Other Christians consult the Bible but interpret it for today's society. They say that, although God inspired the Bible, humans wrote the words down hundreds of years ago to help the society they lived in. Times have changed and God's message needs adapting for the twenty-first century. For instance, attitudes towards women or concern about animals have changed greatly over the past 2000 years.

Other Christians regard the Bible mainly as the source of authority for Church leaders to study and then pass on God's message to worshippers.

### Activity 2

a) Look up the Ten Commandments in Exodus 20:1–17. Briefly list the ten rules.

b) What moral guidance is there for Shelley who is thinking of leaving her husband for a man she met at the gym?

### Activity 3

Make a poster showing the importance of the Bible as a source of authority for Christians.

*The Ten Commandments can be seen on the walls of many churches. This shows how important Christians have found it for making moral decisions.*

**Check you have learnt:**

- why the Bible is an important source of authority
- how a Christian might use the scriptures when making a moral decision
- different attitudes to the authority of the Bible amongst Christians.

**TRY YOUR SKILL AT THIS**

**The (b) question:**

Explain how having a religious faith might influence some believers to use their holy book to make moral decisions. (4)

In this topic you will study some examples of clashes of authority Christians might experience.

# PRIEST RISKS JAIL FOR ASYLUM SEEKER

**1 November 2004**

Father Richard McKay said he was prepared to go to jail if necessary to stop an asylum seeker being deported. Josette Ishimwe was only 13 when she saw her parents and other family members hacked to death in Rwanda. Ten years later she escaped to Britain and in 1994 settled in Bristol. Her request for asylum was turned down; the police and immigration officials turned up to deport her. Josette took refuge in her parish church of St Nicholas of Tolentino and was cared for by fellow parishioners.

Father McKay refused to let officials into the church and said he was prepared to go to prison. "I realize that by stopping them entering I am breaking the law," he said, "but I also have a duty to protect parishioners." He went on to say, "She is a profoundly wounded individual … We are all extremely concerned at the church at what Josette's fate would be if she was sent back to Rwanda."

## Activity 1

Role-play or script an interview between Father McKay and the immigration officials who arrive to deport Josette.

# QUAKERS ARRESTED AT TRIDENT BASE

Ten Quaker protesters were arrested by police for invading the road outside the Faslane Naval Base on Sunday. These Christians, who are pacifists, were protesting against the government's decision to have submarines armed with nuclear warheads. The Quakers believe it is their duty to work towards world peace, which, they say, can never be achieved if a country holds nuclear weapons. Forty Quakers, aged between 16 and 75, held a service of worship outside the gates of the nuclear base and then blocked the road for 15 minutes in quiet protest. Amongst those arrested was 70-year-old Ruth Corry who said, "As a grandmother, I want to make a small contribution to the security of my grandchildren." Another protestor said, "We believe that we should respect the laws of the state, but we believe too that our first loyalty must be to God's purpose."

## Activity 2

Explain what this group of Christians did that was illegal and suggest the religious reasons for their action.

# The extraordinary case of the Doves versus the Hawks

At the dead of night on 29 January 1996, four women broke into the British Aerospace factory at Warton in Lancashire. They slipped past security guards, ran across the runway and managed to force open the doors of an aircraft hangar.

Using ordinary hammers, they smashed the electronics system of a new £12 million Hawk jet waiting to be exported to Indonesia.

After two hours, and more than £1.7 million worth of damage to the plane, they wanted to give themselves up. They tried to flag down a passing police car but when that failed they danced around in front of a close-circuit security camera. Only after a phone call to the Press Association did security guards arrive at 5:00am to arrest them.

In court, the women never denied that they had caused damage to the warplane but they did not plead guilty to criminal damage. They said they damaged the plane to prevent a greater crime of genocide.

*In a decision that surprised most people, the court acquitted these women of criminal damage to a £12 million Hawk jet that they deliberately vandalized.*

They successfully argued that all 24 jets destined for Indonesia were intended for use against innocent civilians in that country's offensive against East Timor. Given Indonesia's record of major human rights abuses and the deaths of 200,000 people (a third of East Timor's population), preventing the export of a jet saved innocent lives.

To many people's astonishment, the jury agreed and acquitted the women.

Andrea Needham, a Catholic and one of the women who damaged the Hawk jet, said:

*"I believe that above all else in life, we are called to love and to be human. I can therefore not stand aside and allow the Hawks to be delivered without doing all that is in my power to peacefully resist. I believe that to be silent in this situation is to be complicit with injustice. I pray that what we do today in disarming these planes will be a small ray of hope for our sisters and brothers struggling for peace and justice in East Timor."*

## Activity 3

Try this (c) question:

> It can never be right to break the law.

Give **two** reasons why a religious believer might agree or disagree with this statement. (4)

**Check you have learnt:**

- at least one example of a clash between the law and personal conviction.

**TRY YOUR SKILL AT THIS**

**The (b) question:**

Explain how having a religious faith might convince a person they must disobey the law of the land. (4)

In this topic you will examine the way some Muslims use the Qur'an as the basis for making moral decisions.

*The Qur'an is always placed on a stand when it is read. By raising the book off the ground, Muslims are showing their respect for the book and its authority.*

## How do Muslims know what is right or wrong?

Like members of other religions, Muslims can turn to their religious leader for advice when it comes to making a moral decision. The imam, who leads the prayers at the mosque, has authority as a religious leader because he has spent many years studying the Qur'an. He can provide Muslims with all the guidance they need about how they should lead the sort of life Allah requires them to.

## Why is the Qur'an the ultimate authority for a Muslim?

Muslims believe that the Qur'an contains everything that humans will ever need to know about how they should lead their lives. The Qur'an is a **revealed book** because the words in it were given to humans by Allah.

The Qur'an was revealed to Prophet Muhammad when he was meditating in a cave outside Makkah. He had a vision of the angel Jibril, who told him to read the words on a fiery scroll. Muhammad could not read, but eventually the message was revealed to him and he learnt it by heart. Over a period of 23 years, Muhammad had more visions in which the angel Jibril revealed to him Allah's message for the whole of humanity. Although Muhammad could not write, his memory was excellent; he recited the words he had learnt to his followers and they carefully wrote them down. This is the Qur'an.

## No translations

Because Allah passed the Qur'an down to Muhammad in Arabic, it can only be read in that language. If it was translated into other languages, errors might creep in and misunderstandings occur. For this reason, no translations of the holy book can be called the Qur'an; they are considered to be interpretations of the holy book.

Most Muslims learn to read some passages from the Qur'an from a very early age, even though Arabic is probably not their native language. Children attend the **madrassah** to learn how to read and recite passages from the Qur'an and, as they grow older, they learn to understand the meaning of these passages.

*The Qur'an provides plenty of guidance about how a person should react if they see people suffering.*

## The straight path

Muslims believe the Qur'an contains all the laws and teachings necessary for life; this is often called the Straight Path. Those who follow the straight path will be led in the right direction through life to Allah. A code of law, known as Shari'ah law, is based directly on the teachings in the Qur'an.

## The Hadith

Muslims do not always find it easy to apply the teachings in the Qur'an to everyday life, and so they turn to **the Hadith**. These writings are based on what Prophet Muhammad said and did. This can be very helpful when Muslims want guidance about applying a Qur'anic teaching to a real-life situation.

## True for all time

Despite the fact that the Qur'an was revealed well over a thousand years ago, Muslims believe that it can never go out of date. Allah knows everything that has happened, is happening and will happen, so the guidance he provides in the Qur'an is perfect. Everything a person needs is there.

### Activity 1

Try this (c) question:

> Scriptures are too old to be of any use today.

Give **two** reasons why a religious believer might agree or disagree with this statement. (4)

### Activity 2

Explain why a Muslim would say that the Qur'an can provide all the moral guidance they need in today's society.

### Check you have learnt:

- why the Qur'an is a revealed book
- why the Qur'an contains all that is necessary for life
- how the Hadith can help Muslims.

### TRY YOUR SKILL AT THIS

The (e) question:

'Reading the holy scriptures will tell a religious believer all they need to know.'

Do you agree? Give reasons or evidence for your answer, showing that you have thought of more than one point of view. You must include reference to religious beliefs in your answer. (8)

# 4.11

## What happens when Muslims experience clashes of authority?

In this topic you will study some examples of clashes of authority Muslims might experience.

## Activity 1

a) Debate the two sides of the Sainsbury's and Mustapha case. How would you have handled it if you were the store manager? Explain your reasons.

b) Explain the problem Mustapha faced. How was it overcome?

Islam treats the subject of alcohol abuse very seriously. The Qur'an forbids the use of alcohol because it can lead to addiction and damage a person's body, as well as the lives of those around them.

# MUSLIMS ALLOWED TO REFUSE TO SELL ALCOHOL

### 30 September 2007

Sainsbury's have agreed that Muslim employees in their supermarkets can refuse to handle alcohol on religious grounds. The case arose when Mustapha, a Muslim checkout worker, told a customer at the checkout that he could not serve him with alcohol because it was against his religion and it was during the holy month of Ramadan.

A spokesperson for Sainsbury's said, 'We try to do our best in terms of complying with the requirements of religions.'

#### The solution

Sainsbury's have said a Muslim can refuse to serve a person with alcohol at the checkout. All they need to do is to raise their hand, in the same way an under-18 checkout operator does for the supervisor's permission to sell drink. In the case of a Muslim, another checkout worker will step in and pass the bottle in front of the scanner.

Sainsbury's have also agreed that Muslims do not have to stack shelves in the wine and spirits section if they do not wish to. Other duties can be given to them.

#### Objections?

This has solved a problem for Muslim employees but some senior Muslims were not happy. The Secretary of the British Muslim Council said, 'People who sell alcoholic beverages cannot be regarded as having sinned. They are just carrying out the requirement of the job in order to earn a living. Muslim employees have a duty to their employer and in supermarkets most people would accept that in selling alcohol you are merely passing it through a checkout. That is hardly going to count against you on the Day of Judgement.'

The director of the Muslim Institute said Sainsbury's was being very good about it but 'the fault lies with the employee who is exploiting and misusing their goodwill'.

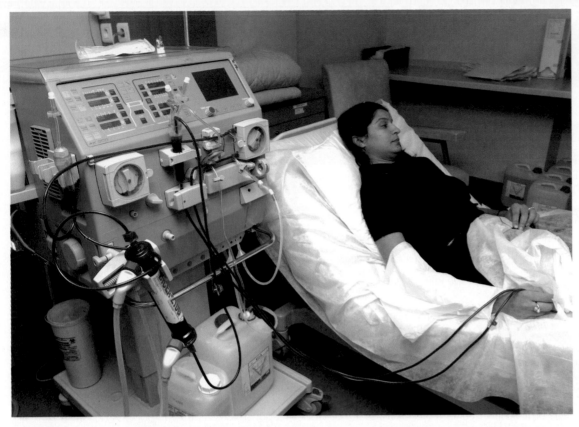

*Dialysis is the process of removing blood from a patient whose kidney functioning is faulty, purifying the blood and returning it to the patient's bloodstream. Patients are usually connected to the haemodialysis machine for 3–4 hours, three times a week. The amount of time spent in hospital or connected to a machine can reduce the patient's independence and quality of life. An alternative for patients with kidney failure is a kidney transplant – this type of transplant can be done from living donors as a person only needs one functioning kidney to survive.*

# DIFFICULT DECISIONS FOR HANIF

Hanif Mohammed has suffered from kidney problems since he was a child, but these got worse in adult life. For the past five years, he has been on kidney dialysis, which has made life difficult for the British Gas employee. As a devout Muslim, Hanif asked his religious leader, the local imam, whether a kidney transplant would be permitted. The imam said, according to his interpretation of the scriptures, Muslims could only accept an organ transplant from a living donor.

The problem arose one evening when Hanif's wife took a call from the hospital to say that they had found a suitable kidney for him from a donor who had recently died. At first, Hanif did not know what to do because he respected the imam he had known for a long time. However, Islam does allow Muslims to ask the opinions of other imams and that was what Hanif did. As a result of talking to others and researching what other Muslim scholars had said, Hanif decided to go ahead and have the transplant.

He has recovered very well and gone on to become a black belt in several martial arts.

30 May 2008

**Check you have learnt:**

- at least one example of a clash of authority that a Muslim has experienced.

## Activity 2

Try this (c) question:

> You have to do what is right for you.

Give **two** reasons why a religious believer might agree or disagree with this statement. (4)

**TRY YOUR SKILL AT THIS**

**The (d) question:**

Explain **two** different examples of how there might be a conflict between personal convictions and authority. (You must state the religious traditions you are referring to.) (6)

## END OF CHAPTER 4 CHECK

### ✓ Check the (a) question

In this chapter *Authority – religion and state* we have explored the impact of authority on religion and society and you have learnt these **KEY CONCEPTS**:

- authority
- duty
- justice
- human rights
- personal conviction
- punishment

a) Write three sentences, each using one of the key concepts from the list above, to show you understand the meaning of three key concepts.

b) Work with a partner to test each other on the meaning of the key concepts in this chapter.

### ✓ Check the (b) question

This is where you will be asked how having a religious faith affects someone's response to an issue. Remind yourself of the Christian and the Muslim response to these issues you have studied, but remember you can use a general religious response if you have good supporting evidence:

- human rights
- the purposes of punishment
- the influence of sacred texts
- conflict between the law of the land and personal conviction.

In each case decide what example you could state and the explanation you would give.

### ✓ Check the (d) question

This question will be asking you to explain the response of two religious traditions to an issue. Make sure you know how Muslims and Christians respond and whether there are any differences within the same religion to these issues:

- teachings about human rights
- beliefs and teachings about punishment
- beliefs and teachings about capital punishment
- beliefs and teachings about authority of holy texts.

### ✓ Check the (c) and (e) questions

The (c) question is where you are offered a controversial statement in a speech bubble to comment on. In (c) questions the examiner is asking you to apply what you know about Christian or Muslim attitudes, or the general attitudes of religious believers, to the issues mentioned above, and to support the points you make with two examples and explanations.

The (e) question is similar but this time gives you a chance to have a say. Obviously, your responses to the issues above do matter. Rehearse some examples you would give to support your viewpoint on each issue and the evidence you would use to support them.

Then revise two or three examples the other side might give with the explanations they would use to argue against you.

Check that you really are clear on the religious viewpoints that might be offered to support or disagree with your view.

## Here are some final handy tips

### BEFORE THE EXAM

☑ Give yourself time to read through your notes quietly.

☑ Look at the Check you have learnt section in the textbook; it gives you a nice quick revision checklist for each topic.

☑ Try some paired testing with a partner.

☑ Get someone to test you on the meaning of the Key concepts or test yourself by writing the words down for each section and making sure you can remember their meanings. Think about other specialist language you have learnt.

☑ Then give yourself a little rest before the exam.

## Now try answering these typical examples of Question 4:

*During* the exam, remember:

☑ Read the whole of each question through before you put pen to paper so you can see exactly what the examiner is asking and where certain information is going to go.

☑ Then spend a few moments looking carefully at the stimulus material and deciding what question each goes with.

☑ As you are writing your answer, bear in mind the sort of question you are answering.

☑ Don't forget the handy **POINT + EXAMPLE + EXPLANATION**.

☑ Include any specialist language that is relevant and any key concepts that fit. Use the stimulus; it's there to give you ideas.

☑ Good luck!

(a) Explain what religious believers mean by 'punishment'. (2)

(b) Explain how having a religious belief influences one person to stand up for human rights. (4)

Holy books are out of date when it comes to giving believers advice.

(c)

Give two reasons why a religious believer might agree or disagree with this statement. (4)

(i)                                                        (ii)

(d) Explain from two different religious teachings about justice.
(You must state the religious tradition you are referring to.) (6)

(i)                                                        (ii)

(e) 'You should always follow your conscience when it comes to moral decisions.'

Do you agree? Give reasons or evidence for your answer, showing that you have thought of more than one point of view. You must include reference to religious beliefs in your answer. (8)

# Key concept glossary

| | |
|---|---|
| **authority** | right or power over others |
| **community** | a group of people who are joined together because they share something in common |
| **conflict** | clashes and breakdowns of relationships |
| **conscience** | an innate moral sense that guides actions and responses |
| **duty** | something you do because it is the accepted pattern of behaviour |
| **evangelism** | spreading a faith or religion to others |
| **faith** | to have trust or confidence |
| **free will** | the belief that nothing is determined |
| **Hippocratic Oath** | a special promise made by those working in medicine to do their best to preserve life |
| **human rights** | something a person is entitled to because they are human |
| **identity** | the sense of who you are in terms of attitudes, character and personality |
| **interfaith dialogue** | exploring common grounds between different faith groups |
| **justice** | where everyone has equal provisions and opportunity |

| | |
|---|---|
| **just war** | a war undertaken to protect the innocent or those being violated and to restore justice and peace |
| **medical ethics** | the moral principles that affect medical issues and practice |
| **non-violent protest** | showing disapproval without damaging property or causing any threat |
| **pacifism** | the belief that any form of violence or war is unacceptable |
| **personal conviction** | something a person strongly feels or believes in |
| **pilgrimage** | a form of spiritual adventure |
| **punishment** | a penalty given to someone for a crime or wrong they have done |
| **quality of life** | the extent to which life is meaningful and pleasurable |
| **reconciliation** | bringing harmony to a situation of disagreement and discord |
| **sacred** | something to be revered or respected above other things |
| **sanctity of life** | life is precious and utterly priceless |

## What the examiner said

What the examiner said about Chan's answer to the (d) question on **page 76**:

*Chan has shown a good understanding of the two religions he chose. He gained Level 3 because he has given several brief examples but not developed any of them sufficiently enough to go up to Level 4. If Chan had written, 'They pray five times a day and read the Qur'an to get closer to Allah.' and developed his point about Christian Aid to say, 'Helping the poor is what Jesus asks of Christians.', he could have moved up to Level 4.*

What the examiner said about Sonja's answer to the (c) question on **page 77**:

*Sonja has written an excellent 4 mark answer. Each point she makes is backed up with a reason and an example from the religion. I have to admit that I was very impressed by the fact that she could show the reasons for and against this statement and link it to two religions. However, Sonja could still have achieved full marks with statements from one religion that totally agreed or disagreed with the statement.*

What the examiner said about Neil's answer to the (d) question on **page 116**:

*Neil started his answer off well, giving a basic statement which he developed and offered two well-developed examples. This took him up to Level 3 and I awarded him 4 marks. But when it came to explaining the attitude of another religion, there was nothing to reward in his answer. Neil needed to state what Christians think and then develop his argument with examples. Sadly he did none of that.*